THE HORN

THE
HORN

Kurt Janetzky and Bernhard Brüchle

Translated from the German by
James Chater

B.T. Batsford · London

Translated from the German edition
© 1977 Hallwag AG Bern, assigned to B. Schott's Söhne, Mainz

ISBN 0 7134 5681 7

Typeset by Servis Filmsetting Ltd, Manchester
Printed in Great Britain by
The Bath Press, Bath
for the publisher
B.T. Batsford Ltd
4 Fitzhardinge Street
London W1H 0AH

Published simultaneously with this volume

The Trumpet
Edward Tarr

The Oboe and the Bassoon
Gunther Joppig

The Flute
Raymond Meylan

Jacket Illustration
Inventionshorn with bell painted by Courtois, Paris, c 1820. On the outer bell rim are engraved the words: ***COURTOIS NEVEU AINE RUE DES VIEUX AUGUSTINS A PARIS***

The horn was still in use in the Paris Opera until about 1850 and today is in the possession of Harold Meek, Newark, Ohio, USA

Painted horns originate mainly from French instrument-builders of the first half of the nineteenth century and are usually decorated with floral patterns, Classical ornamentation with musical motives or chinoiserie. Because of severe wear and tear in the course of playing, only a few well preserved examples are still known

Contents

Introduction

 . . . In concert-halls and opera-houses, the Waldhorn-player can be called upon to express countless things. He can be effective at a distance or near at hand. Charm and (so to speak) a friendly sadness provide the essential tone of this splendid instrument. For echo, no instrument is more capable or more suitable than the horn. A study of this instrument is therefore to be most strongly recommended to any composer . . .

Seldom have the words of a writer on aesthetics been so widely accepted; even more seldom was it so rewarding to follow their recommendation. In 1784, the year in which Christian Friedrich Daniel Schubart (1739–91) wrote them in his *Versuch einer Ästhetik der Tonkunst*, the horn was by no means a 'new' instrument. From 1713 until the middle of the century, Johann Mattheson (1681–1764) and other noted music theorists asserted in several of their essays, in almost amusingly exact word-for-word agreement, that the 'the lovely, majestic Waldhorn has nowadays become very fashionable'. But this can mean only that the original horn, the earliest signal-instrument in the history of mankind, and later the legendary symbol of chivalry, which long before the Romantic period had already become indispensible to all hunters, postilions and night watchmen, was beginning to evolve into the musical instrument now taken for granted throughout the musical world.

What music-lover could help being entranced by the three horn notes that open the overture to Weber's *Oberon* with such a wonderfully magical effect? We are drawn irresistibly by their spell and lured into an enchanted world of elves and fairies. Who would not be stirred and cheered by the sound of the morning call, full of the joys of nature, with which the two orchestral horns, softly and with restraint, yet with a telling sense of urgency, intone the opening of the solemn 'Introitus' to Franz Schubert's 'Great' C major Symphony? Who would not be carried

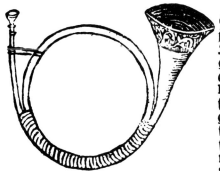

Die lieblich - pompeusen Wald-Hörner, ital. Cornete di Caccia, Call. Cors de Chasse, sind bey ietziger Zeit sehr en vogue kommen, so wohl was Kirchen- als Theatral - und Cammer-Music anlanget, weil sie theils nicht so rude von Natur sind, als die Trompeten, theils auch, weil sie mit mehr Facilité können tractirt werden. Die brauchbarsten haben f und mit den Trompeten aus dem c gleichen Ambitum. Sie klingen auch dicker, und füllen besser aus, als die schreyende Clarinen, weil sie um eine ganze Quint tiefer stehen. Wiewohl man heutiges Tags auch C. Wald-Hörner hat, welche eine völlige Octav tiefer sind als die Trompeten. Uber dieses können solche auch mit Setz Stücken und Krum-Bögen höher und tiefer gestimmt werden,

From Joseph Friedrich Bernhard Casper Majer (1689–1768), Neu-eröffneter Theoretisch- und Pracktischer Music-Saal, *Schwäbisch Hall, 1732 and Nuremberg, 1741*

The text had already appeared practically word-for-word in Johann Mattheson (1681–1764) in Das neu-eröffnete Orchestre, *Hamburg, 1713 and in Johann Philipp Eisel (1698–after 1756),* Musicus autodidaktos, oder der sich selbst informirende Musicus, *Erfurt, 1738*

expectantly away when, in any of the world's opera houses, Giuseppe Verdi opens his rendering of the bloody story of the hapless Infante Don Carlos with the dull gleam of four horns, like the splendid illumination at the beginning of some medieval manuscript? Who would be unwilling, after hearing the E flat chords on eight horns surging above the 136-bar pedal-point crescendo during the introduction of *Das Rheingold*, to place himself in Richard Wagner's hands?

The expressive potential of the horn is inexhaustible, its scope for musical urgency and persuasion limitless. And composers knew how to exploit it: Agricola (1720–74), Jommelli (1714–74) and especially Gluck (1714–87) were among those who did (as Schubart in fact wrote) with overwhelming power and effect.

Long before this, the horn aroused boisterous high spirits in every true huntsman, while its joyous hunting-calls spurred the company on to vigorous, happy hunting. But at the same time skilled musicians were taking to the instrument, and it was soon used, with astonishing, song-like beauty, by Baroque musicians and many composers of the pre-Classical and early Classical eras, as a vehicle for genuine emotional expression. Eventually, during the expansive, many-sided period from Classicism to Romanticism, countless major and minor composers came to consider it indispensible and suitable 'for every musical mood'; it was often the clearly favoured and favourite instrument.

And so it remained, to be enhanced still further by the revolutionary invention of the valve. Only with these new, hitherto unsuspected possibilities was it able to conquer the heights of mid- and late-Romantic orchestral sound. Even the most modern exponents of the new, realistic school still regarded the traditional horn as a staunch ally; even the sober, functional innovators are unwilling or unable to do without its vigorous, masculine sound.

With its mild, velvety chordal sound, the Waldhorn is capable of providing a harmonious accompaniment and reliable support to the softest vocal or instrumental solo; and equally it can seize the initiative by surging boldly above the wild torrents of sound in the outsize orchestras of Richard Strauss or Gustav Mahler; every music-lover would therefore profit from a closer knowledge of the instrument. The purpose of this short book is to rescue the instrument from the anonymity of the orchestra and to provide a concise history of its development and function.

Bronze medal (1975) by Elizabeth Jones. Front side: Wolfgang Amadeus Mozart (1756–91). Reverse side: Waldhorn with detachable crook (end of eighteenth century)

ONE

Origins and Prehistory

The first horn sounds must have been produced long before mankind started to count the years. We do not know how, where or when this happened, though we can assume it was in the East, in distant prehistoric times. No doubt it was by chance that one of our ancestors happened to come across a section of tube of the kind nature could provide directly. Perhaps it was the shell of a marine snail, perhaps the hollow bone of an animal that had perished or been struck down, perhaps just the hollow stem of a dried-up piece of sea-weed, or even the horn of a buffalo, bison, ram or bull, hollowed out by the effects of time, broken off at the top or pierced at the side.* It is easy to imagine how one of these men, fishing on some southern shore or hunting on the blazing steppes of Africa or Asia, might have placed such a pipe to his lips out of a child-like impulse, in order to puff away any remaining water, pulp or accumulated sand. If he did this with tensed lips and roughly in the manner that modern players call 'embouchure', then his lips, acting like vibrating blades, must unexpectedly have transferred these same vibrations to the air column enclosed by the tube. According to natural acoustical laws a sound must have been generated that, in terms of height or depth, timbre and intensity, depended as much on the length and

* In mythology, legends, literature and art, even in specialist literature on instruments and modern scores, we frequently encounter the term 'Muschelhorn'. For zoological and technical reasons, no wind instrument could possibly be made from a bivalved, or two-piece shell (*Muschel*). Only snails (*Schnecken*) have a shell consisting of a single, helical structure from which horns can be made. These cannot be called 'trumpets', because their conical tube cannot be disputed. The instrument termed *Muschelhorn* or *Muscheltrompete* is thus a *Schneckenhorn*. [*Translator's note*: the term *(See)schnecke* is translated as '(marine) snail', the term *Schneckenhorn* by 'conchhorn'. In strict zoological terms, a 'conch' is a marine snail of the Gastropoda class (subclass Prosobranchia), or the shell in which it is housed. By extension, the word 'conch' is used to denote any enclosed, helical shell adapted or adaptable as a musical instrument.]

Conch-horn player, Papua New Guinea

Rana-cringa player, Indian figurine

form of the tube as on the tension of the lips and the strength of the player's lungs.

Thus a primitive pipe evolved into an instrument, and at the same time the horn came into being. This event, wherever and whenever it took place, must immediately have enhanced the rank and stature of the 'inventor', earning him astonished admiration and awe from every member of his tribe. Perhaps the sound of the horn, never heard before and therefore considered magic and miraculous, had such an effect that the person who knew how to produce it was elevated to the rank of chieftain, priest or even of a god.

Early Forms in Antiquity, in the East and Elsewhere

The oldest conch-horns to be used as wind instruments may have been of Assyrian origin or derived from the pre-Aryan Indus civilization. Some very rare specimens were to be found in the collection of Francis William Galpin (1859–1945), perhaps the leading organologist and champion of comparative musicology in England. He suspected that they were most probably for cultic use and derived from the period around 2000 to 1500 BC.

From Greek mythology we know the conch-horn, blown by Triton, son of the sea-god Poseidon and Amphitrite. It is not particularly surprising if, in the southern Pacific and on several other southern shores, similar horns made from the shells of marine snails have often been found, with or without the addition of small bamboo pipes resembling mouthpieces or other metal blowing devices. However, their spread, along with that of imitations constructed from clay or alabaster, can be demonstrated by archaeological finds made at sites far from the sea, for

10

*Kudu-horn player,
South-West Africa*

*Terracotta horn in
the form of a
jaguar, Peru,
early Mochica art*

instance in Peru and Mexico. A particularly interesting conch-horn, made from the shell of the Fasciolara gigantea and called *tecciztli* or *quiquiztli*, was used by priests of ancient Mexico to invoke the rain-gods. And many parallels can be established in many ancient and primitive societies from all parts of the world.

Horn instruments made from the hollowed-out horns or bored-through tusks of animals are much more common. They too can be found throughout the world; indeed, in the thirteenth and fourteenth centuries travellers in Africa reported the use for peaceful purposes of antelopes' and cows' horns as instruments among shepherds in areas of Ethiopa; but, in the hands of a few tribes in Sudan, Congo and other parts of eastern Africa the same instrument usually emitted a strongly menacing, openly warlike roar.

Giant mammoths, elephants from Africa and India, buffaloes from the Far East (Tibet, Siam, Bengal and Nepal) and bulls from South America (Brazil and Argentina) must also have yielded tusks and horns that were adapted, in all their variety, as wind instruments to be used by people in their prayers for rain and fertility; these instruments were used in the celebration of feasts, but also summoned hunters and warriors to perform bloodthirsty acts, assisting them with various signals that could be heard at a distance.

The ancient Jewish *shofar* is already well known from the Bible, both for its trombone-like sound, powerful enough to break down walls without resistance, and as a ritual instrument. A ram's horn without a mouthpiece, it not only caused the fortifications of Jericho to crumble, but is also still used in the Judaic Rite of the Levites at new moon, and for the solemn proclamation of the Day of Atonement and at the New Year. Skilled artisans from China,

11

Rana-cringa, a painted copper war-horn from India. It has a piercing sound, causing lead pellets inside the dividing rings to rattle. Length: 1.47 metres (The Metropolitan Museum of Art, the Crosby Brown Collection, 1889, New York)

India and Tibet, and also from the Near East, using natural models, fashioned richly adorned imitations of horns from bronze, copper, pewter and brass. Today many of these instruments are valuable museum pieces, true monuments, in a cultural sense, to the ancient art of metal-work.

All these instruments were still severely limited in their performance capabilities. Most could give only a single note, some perhaps two or at most three. Their 'musical' use must therefore have been almost always limited to the repetition of signals distinguishable only through their rhythm.

Etruscan Horns, Signal-horns (Bugles) in Ancient Rome; Lurs in Northern Europe

It was probably in the seventh century BC that the Etruscans migrated from south-western Asia Minor to central Italy. They

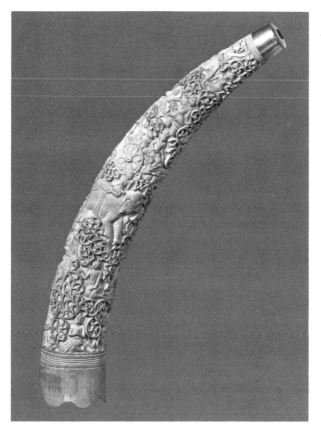

Left: *Richly decorated ivory horn from Burma. Length: 30 cm (The Metropolitan Museum of Art, the Crosby Brown Collection, 1889, New York)*

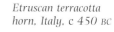

Brazilian bull-horn

Below left: *Watchman sounding the horn on the Great Wall of china (c second century BC)*
Below right: *Rabbi sounding the shofar, after a Rothschild manuscript, Italy c 1470*

Etruscan terracotta horn, Italy, c 450 BC

established themselves relatively near Rome and became indigenous to the later province of Etruria. To their new land they brought not only Greek influences but also the Etruscan horn. This was fashioned, crudely but effectively, from terracotta. Its harsh tone was quite loud and carried an astonishingly long way. Its most remarkable feature, however, was its semicircular form, which lasted for several centuries. We encounter it again in numerous French and German hunting-horns of the seventeenth and eighteenth centuries; then it was made of metal and called a *Halbmond* (crescent or half-moon). For a time it was used by companies of Bavarian huntsmen, and horn-players in the traditional battalions of the Hamburg town militia still carried them until the middle of the nineteenth century.

It was inevitable that two cultures as developed as those of Etruria and its neighbour, ancient Rome, exerted a mutual influence and intermingled; and almost equally that the expanding Roman empire soon confronted the Etruscans as enemies. And yet it took two centuries for Rome to conquer and subdue the Etruscans. In that time the well-organized system of Roman military signals developed. Among the instruments used in this system we again find the *cornu*, which had been taken over from the Etruscans. The Romans very soon learnt to fashion it from metal, including its characteristic handle. In addition we find the *lituus*, resembling the Celtic carnyx, and the *tuba*, absolutely indispensible for solemn funerals, and the deep-toned *cornu*, whose players always marched at the head of the procession. The most imposing of all these instruments was the powerful *buccina*: this was a brass horn more than three metres long, wound almost into a circle and originally the signal horn of seafarers, sailors and shepherds. It must have had great performance capabilities, for several representations on mosaics, vases and vessels used for drinking or for ornamental purposes show that the buccina

Left: Cornu-*player, Trajan's column, Rome, 117* AD. Centre: *Organist,* tuba
-*player and two* buccina-*players, after a fragment of the Amphitheatre mosaic in
Zliten,* c *70* AD. Right: Lur *from the Nordic Bronze Age, Denmark,* c *1000* BC *(?)*

found many uses as an accompanimental instrument – even
during circus acts and gladiator fights. These objects carry
depictions, for the most part very realistic, of the instruments and
their players, working singly or in pairs, occasionally even
accompanied on the organ and the long tuba.

Comparable to the buccina, but still completely independent
from it, is the Bronze Age *lur*. Examples could be found, usually in
pairs next to each other, at excavations of early German
settlements in Scandinavia and northern Germany in the course
of the last century. They were so well preserved in the marshy
districts where they lay sunk, for perhaps as long as two or even
three thousand years, that they came to light almost completely
undamaged. They all have in common a superbly balanced form.
The tubes, two to three metres in length, form a symmetrical pair
resembling the tusks of a mammoth and are finely curved in an S-
shape or in the form of a question-mark. The quality of the
craftsmanship is astonishing. The wonderfully thin-walled,
gently tapered conical tube is cast in several pieces from bronze.
The thin parts are then skilfully joined and so firmly bound

together by ornamental bands that the whole instrument appears as though moulded seamlessly from a single cast. The bell section is a flat, usually finely decorated, ornamental disc. The mouthpiece is almost exactly like that of a modern tenor trombone.

What was played on these horn instruments has nowhere been recorded. From a musical point of view, the performance capabilities of the buccina and lur were already considerable; moreover, the twinned instruments were in complete agreement as to timbre and tuning. However, this by no means proves that they were used for two-voice music. We can probably assume that they were played in unison or in alternation, but still only in one part.

The craft of forming or moulding such thin-walled, conical tubes from metal was lost in the upheavals caused by mass migration. Only in the Middle Ages was it reinvented and relearnt, and then with great difficulty.

Oliphants and Gold Horns from Tondern

Harun Ar-Rashid, celebrated for his legendary virtue, reigned in Baghdad from 786 to 809 as fifth caliph of the Abbāsid dynasty. He is reputed to have presented to Charlemagne the ivory horn still preserved in the cathedral treasury at Aix-la-Chapelle. It is an elephant's tusk, richly adorned with carvings and skilfully hollowed out – an oliphant similar to the very luxurious items that reached Europe from Byzantium in relatively large numbers from about the tenth century. Its great value meant that only the nobility and men of rank could use them as hunting-horns. Soon they became the exalted symbols of medieval chivalry, were treated as the badges of earned honours and were sometimes even conferred in place of formal deeds of loan. Their withdrawal,

Right: *The so-called 'hunting-horn of Charles the Great', an oriental* Hifthorn *from the cathedral treasure at Aix-la-Chapelle. Arc width: 58 cm. Diameter of the bell opening: 13 cm. Probably from Lower Italy, it is presumed not to have originated until around 1000*

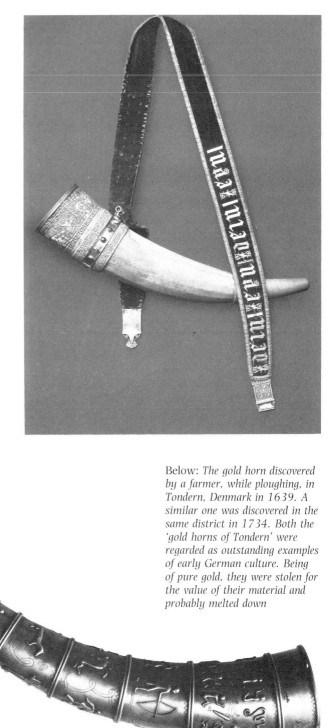

Below: *The gold horn discovered by a farmer, while ploughing, in Tondern, Denmark in 1639. A similar one was discovered in the same district in 1734. Both the 'gold horns of Tondern' were regarded as outstanding examples of early German culture. Being of pure gold, they were stolen for the value of their material and probably melted down*

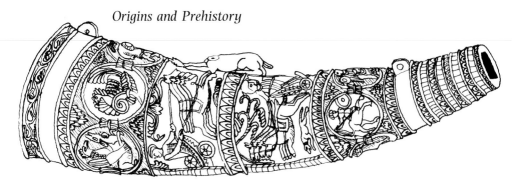

One of the precious oliphants from the knightly entourage of Charles the Great (742–814)

like the loss of a sword, brought shame and dishonour and was considered a disgrace.

Such an oliphant plays a part in the *Chanson de Roland*, the greatest of the courtly-chivalric epics. After his campaign against the Saracens in Spain in 778, Roland, the nephew and follower of Charlemagne, had to bring up the rear during the retreat through the western Pyrenees. Separated from the main army, he and his men were ambushed by a vast Moorish hoard and almost completely cut to pieces. Finally, Roland seized his horn and called to Charles for help. He blew with such superhuman strength that 'the blood sprang bright-red from his mouth'. Charlemagne, already deep into Gascony, heard it, for its tone 'carried a good 30 miles'. The mountains resounded with 60,000 answering trumpets, but as Charles reached the battlefield it was already too late. Roland struck another Saracen with the oliphant and died, his glazed eyes turned towards Spain.

The oliphant blown by the mortally wounded knight Roland before his death has passed into legend. In other contemporary epics too, oliphants are often mentioned and play poetically meaningful roles. Along with many other famous oliphants that belonged to persons of rank who attained historical significance, Roland's horn was naturally coveted by many famous art collections for its value and rarity. It is therefore not surprising if, for example, the oliphant reputedly sounded by St Hubert, patron saint of huntsmen, or the one owned by the Polish king Jan III Sobyesky (1624–96), turned up in various places at the same time. The confusion became even greater when similar copies appeared on the market. Many of them found takers who paid well, and very often it was extremely difficult even for the experts to distinguish originals from clever forgeries.

A truly incalculable loss resulted from a theft which even today has not been cleared up: in 1639 and in 1734, in ploughed fields near Tondern, Denmark, farmers found two horns made of pure gold. Both had designs of outstanding artistic significance and were testament to Early High German culture. They were both stolen. Fortunately, however, we possess very clear drawings and detailed descriptions of them, made directly after their discovery. The precious objects, which fell into the hands of thieves still unidentified, were probably melted down without regard for their cultural and art-historical value.

The Signal-horns of Night Watchmen, Firemen, Türmer, Hunting-serfs, Shepherds, Bakers, Butchers and Early Postilions

In the centuries when aristocratic knights often bore their precious oliphants only for show, as a visible symbol of their nobility, rather than for playing, many other types of horn were frequently used.

In towns, *Türmer* (tower watchmen) and night watchmen used them to sound the hour, warn of danger and to report the outbreak of any fires. In the flat countryside and villages, the horns of local shepherds would summon cattle from their stalls early in the morning, collect them into herds and drive them into the pastures. Bakers, particularly in the Netherlands, used horn signals to spread the news that their wares could once again be had fresh from the oven, or to tell housewives that the oven had again been heated and that they could bring to the bakery the dough they had prepared at home.

In several regions, especially Swabia in Germany, butchers' lads merrily sounded their horns to announce their readiness to convey news and letters as they rushed from place to place in their waggons. This was the *Metzgerpost* (butchers' post), which became respected and cherished; those who ran it were the early precursors of the postilions.

Left: *Flemish baker*
Copper engraving of 1748 after
a painting by A. van Ostade,
from the German Bread
Museum, Ulm

Right: *Alphorn-player, after a lithograph*
of Bacler d'Albe, 1818

To start with, all these people would have blown simple cow-horns of various sizes. Wealthy towns with large cathedrals or churches and town halls gave their *Türmer* compact, thick-walled watchmen's horns made of heavy metal and modelled on the horn of a very large bull. Thus for example the bronze *Grüselhorn*, cast by a fifteenth-century founder and blown from the tower of the minster in Strasbourg, or the impressive watchman's horn, likewise of bronze or copper, blown by the *Türmer* of St Lambert's, Münster, Münsterland and in St Mary's in the ancient Hanseatic town of Rostock. The gold *Harsthorn*, used in the town of Lucerne from as early as about 1455, may still, because of its elegant form, have been extremely rare in the Middle Ages. In contrast the small, often very beautiful metal horns carried by princely hunt attendants and hunting serfs produced nothing more than a primitive toot and so scarcely merited the name of *Hifthorn* (hunting-horn). The servants merely carried out menial hunting tasks or functioned as beaters, and their instruments are not to be confused with those of the aristocratic hunters who had been trained for the chase. Whatever their size, most of these instruments could play only one or at most two notes. In fact, the pitch and timbre of these notes often depended on the length and bore-size of the horn being used.

Shepherds' Horns and the Swiss Alphorn

Some wooden horns were already far superior to the metal horns of the time, and their performance capabilities were, from a 'musical' standpoint, considerably better.

If the construction of thin-walled, predominantly conical metal tubes was still absolutely unknown in the cultivated circles of central Europe, the instinct of the amateur craftsman must have prompted shepherds to make such a tube from a small grown tree for use as a wind instrument.

In Switzerland folk memories of the Celtic carnyx or Roman lituus may have played a role in inspiring such trains of thought. In any case, Conrad Gesner, a scholar of Zürich, refers to the alphorn as the 'lituum alpinum' as early as 1555. In the Balkans, Austria, Saxony, Thuringia and Bavaria, a few of the slender, gently curved, conical shepherds' horns were in use at that time. Also in distant Ethiopa and among the Arauca, Queshua and Aymara Indians of South America we find wind instruments that are remarkably similar to the Swiss alphorn.

Both the shepherd's horn and the alphorn were constructed in various sizes, usually from naturally grown fir. Longitudinally halved, each half was carefully hollowed and reunited with the other half, both then being firmly glued together. The whole tube was then surrounded by strips of willow bark or braid, as well as a

21

Horn in F   *Ludwig van Beethoven, from Symphony No. 6, Op. 68*

Corno di pastore in G

Allegro moderato   Leopold Mozart

protective coat of varnish. The mouthpiece, made from box-tree, was usually turned on a lathe or skilfully carved.

By their very nature, shepherds' horns and alphorns are genuine horn instruments. Both have a decidely popular character, but both received tributes in symphonic music. Beethoven paid his tribute in the 'Shepherds' Song' from the last movement of his 'Pastoral' Symphony. An aural memory, either real or imaginary, inspired him to use a melody typical of the shepherd's horn to express 'happy, grateful feelings after the storm'. However, in the symphony, this solo is played by the first Waldhorn-player of the orchestra, not on a genuine shepherd's horn.

Brahms used the beautiful melody played by an alphorn-player near the Stockhorn on 12 September 1868 as the pathos-laden, passionate C-horn solo in the finale of his First Symphony. He notated these bars on a postcard, which he sent to Clara Schumann for her birthday, adding the observation:

Thus sounded the alphorn today:

Adagio

In folk-music we naturally find frequent traces of the alphorn. Swiss alphorn-calls like this, with their typical passages in echo, are basic elements of Alpine folk-music culture.

Leopold Mozart, in his *Sinfonia pastorella* in G, wrote a pretty piece for strings and 'corno di pastore' or 'corno pastoritio', the

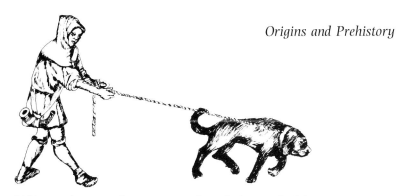

Picking up the scent, after a miniature from the hunting-book by Gaston III (called Phoebus), Conte de Foix, c 1380

solo part of which, for alphorn or shepherd's horn, exploits the instrument in a particularly interesting and charming manner.

Richard Wagner, too, turned to alphorns, as much for their Swiss origin as for their novel tone colour, when, during his time of poverty and distress in Paris, he accepted commissions to write an orchestral work using Swiss folk-melodies and music for a vaudeville, *La descente de la courtille*.

The shepherd's horn has been obsolete for a long time. Only a few instruments, preserved as museum pieces, remain in working order. The alphorn, on the contrary, has undergone a welcome renaissance. Today, in Switzerland, it is once again treated almost as a national symbol: enthusiastic amateurs venerate it, folk-musicians cultivate it and professional artists derive pleasure from it, sometimes playing it with great virtuosity. Some present-day Swiss composers, such as Paolo Baratto, André Besançon, Jean Daetwyler, Etienne Isoz and others, have written sophisticated concert-hall music for the alphorn.

Hunting-horns

> *Praise him with the sound of the trumpet:*
> *Praise him with the psaltery and harp.*

So runs the third verse of Psalm 150, with its exhortation to thank and praise God in song, dance and music. This same psalm, more than any other, inspired many miniaturists and illuminators, mostly anonymous, to depict medieval musicians with joyful, colourful paintings on parchment. Although the other verses of this psalm mention only drums, pipes, stringed instruments and cymbals, in almost all psalters from the ninth to the thirteenth centuries contain a striking number of very realistic depictions of hunting-horn players.

23

Hunters with single-loop horns, after La Vénerie *(1573) by Jacques Du Fouilloux (1521–73)*

Hunting-horns were also mentioned in literature very early on. As early as the twelfth century, in the *Roman d'Alixandre*, a small, metal horn from early France called an 'araine' is mentioned, and in the early versions of the *Chanson de Roland* the use of a small, strident hunting-horn called a 'graile' is described.

Many more, far clearer references to hunting-horns can be found in very early books, particularly instruction books for hunting. Perhaps the oldest of these are *Le dit de la chace dou cerf*, a French treatise from about 1260 in the form of a dialogue of 500 rhymed verses, *L'art de vénerie*, whose author, Guillaume Twici, was master of the hunt at the English court, and which became known around 1315, and *Le livre du Roy Modus* of 1330.

By far the most important of these books is the *Le livre du trésor de vanerie* by Hardouin de Fontaines-Guérin (1394). In nearly 2000 verses and a series of attractive woodcarvings, he describes the highlights of the contemporary hunt. Information about various situations in the hunt and about the events associated with them could be conveyed to the scattered huntsmen by means of 14 distinct signals that reverberated a long way off. The rhythmic sequence of notes and the respective lengths of the individual horn calls were impressed on the mind, in a system comparable to modern Morse code, by means of black and white rectangles, indicating long and short notes respectively, placed at the upper borders of the individual pictures. Without doubt it was a masterly achievement to retain all these in one's memory and use them correctly in the heat of the chase.

A later hunting-book, still French, but printed in Paris in 1573, is *La vénerie* by Jacques du Fouilloux. He already distinguishes horns with high and low notes and also includes a fine woodcut depicting hunters using small horns, evidently made of metal and coiled in a circular loop.

Musical and organological experts, however, tend to be much

German hunting-serf, after a glass painting of the early sixteenth century

more reserved in their pronouncements concerning the horn. The first to mention it at all is Sebastian Virdung (*c* 1500); this he does in his treatise *Musica getutscht* (Basle, 1511) in a highly disparaging way, declaring that the 'Jegerhorn' and 'Acherhorn' were suitable only for 'larking about' ('für göckel spill'). Michael Praetorius (1571–1621), in his *Theatrum instrumentorum* (Wolfenbüttel, 1620), reproduces some hunting-horns and two single-loop horns in true-to-scale diagrams. The Parisian Marin Mersenne (1588–1648), a highly learned Pauline, made frequent and relatively detailed mention of the hunting-horn in several of his exhaustive treatises on music theory. He was already acquainted with horns of varying size, among these horns of up to two metres in length. He also indicates that it is possible to produce well-sounding triads, always providing that the tuning of each horn can be made compatible with those of the other instruments, like the pipes of an organ. The consorts of four or more instruments that he describes are probably only theoretical or are to be understood as wishful, if prophetic thinking. Nowhere does he elaborate on these with musical quotations or other details. In any event, however, the first step appears to have been taken in turning the simple hunting-horn, with its arbitrary single note, into a horn capable of playing one or more precisely determined notes. Thus was fulfilled the most important precondition for turning a primitive signal-instrument (or bugle) into a hunting instrument that could be used in a 'musical' way; this development was brought about by the hunt.

TWO

Early Experiments, New Discoveries, Development and Progress

Let us summarize the story so far. The horn could have originated anywhere there was human life. The natural origins of the materials used – conches, plants, bones, tusks and horns – and the fact that throughout the world ancient civilizations grew up without contact with or even knowledge of one another leads one to suspect that everywhere inventions and discoveries are being made repeatedly. No race or nation, and certainly no individual can claim the honour of making the first discovery. Naturally, the development manifested itself differently in each place. Just occasionally we find some proof of astonishing workmanship and high artistic finish in the form of exotic horns or horn instruments from early times and remote countries. Their players have remained unknown and the societies to which they belonged have become extinct, perhaps in the same way as the Roman Empire along with its bronze buccinas; or perhaps their instruments have sunk into marshland, like the Bronze-Age and early German lurs. Not a single one of the horn instruments of ancient times survived the turmoil of migration to provide an example or prototype. In medieval Europe, mankind arrived at a completely new beginning. It took him decades, if not centuries, to raise the primitive, one-note watchman's horn and the essentially similar hunting-horn to a higher level of evolution and to create a hunting-horn that could play more notes, or the Waldhorn, which could play several.

This was made possible only with completely new scientific knowledge and newly acquired craftmanship: the discovery and exploitation of the law of the harmonic series, and the eventual discovery of the the technique of manufacturing long metal tubes that could be coiled at will. We will deal with these two discoveries in the following sections.

Numbering according to overtones

Numbering according to partials

Notes with minus signs (−) (17, 13 and 14) are a little too low; the eleventh partial (+) lies between F and F sharp, thus a little too high for F, a little too low for F sharp

The Harmonic Series

In its essentials, the natural harmonic series cannot have been unknown to the ancient Greeks, but Marin Mersenne, the Parisian priest we mentioned earlier, is considered to have discovered it. He found that, with each single note of sufficient dynamic strength, other notes (overtones) sounded softly yet audibly. These overtones were contained in each fundamental note like the colours of the spectrum; they originated through simple and direct multiplication of the vibrations of the fundamental note. The sympathetic vibration and sounding of these overtones occurred in a wholly predetermined order founded on natural laws. If these sympathetically sounding 'partials' were systematically reconstructed in their correct order, the above harmonic or 'overtone' series was obtained. The scientist Joseph Sauveur (1653–1716), an outstandingly gifted mathematician and physicist, attempted to explain the harmonic series for the first time in his *Principes d'acoustique et de musique* (1701). Generations of scholars, among them Johann Bernoulli (1667–1748) and Daniel Bernoulli (1700–81) (both from the great dynasty of mathematicians), Ernst Florens Friedrich Chadini (1756–1827) and many others, including Hermann von Helmholtz (1821–94) and Werner Lottermoser (b. 1909) in modern times have been preoccupied with these and other related problems involving acoustics, physics and mathematics.

Tone Production and the Acoustics of the Horn

The tone production and acoustical processes of the horn are essentially the same as for all other brass instruments. The art of playing, however, resides less in directing the air current through the tube than in the correct 'lipping'. The tensed lips are set in vibration by the air current. The tone itself is pushed out by the

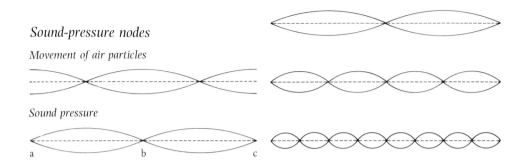

Sound-pressure nodes

Movement of air particles

Sound pressure

a　　　　　　　　b　　　　　　　　c

sudden withdrawal of the tip of the tongue from the crack between the lips, almost as if one were trying to puff a piece of grain from the tongue. The lips are like two cushions which vibrate both to and fro and back and forth, in other words, three-dimensionally. This kind of tone production is considerably more complex than in the case of flutes, reeds (oboe, clarinet, bassoon) or organ pipes.

No less complex are the acoustical processes of the horn; here they can be presented only in a crudely over-simplified form. Through the vibration of the lips, the air current is periodically interrupted, so that pockets of air compression and rarefaction are formed in the air column inside the horn. However, compression (higher sound pressure) means at the same time that the individual air particles have less room in which to vibrate. In areas of low sound pressure, on the contrary, the movement of the particles is stronger. The spread of the vibrations outwards to adjacent air particles may be compared to the fanning out of a ripple on the surface of water after a stone has been thrown into it.

In the diagram, two peaks of pressure lie between nodes *a*, *b* and *c*. Such a sequence is called a wave. The exact way in which these waves are generated and how they are stored in the horn will not be further described here because of the complexity of the subject. The specialist reader will find more details in the literature mentioned in the bibliography (Aebi, Boegner, Meyer). However the elementary relationship between wave length and harmonic series is important. If, for example, you divide a sounding violin string in half by pressing on the middle of it with your finger, it will sound an octave higher than the original note. The same thing happens if you halve the wavelength in a vibrating air column. You can either divide the tube length in half or 'overblow' into the same tube by an octave. In the latter case the

28

air column vibrates in two wavelengths. A further halving or quartering of the original length produces a sound respectively one or two octaves higher. The relationship of notes an octave apart is thus based on the ratio 1:2. If we assign the number 1 to the fundamental, the first note in the natural harmonic series, and the numbers 2, 3, 4 etc. to the following partials in the series, the resulting ratios correspond exactly to the ratios of the wavelengths. The same applies for the ratios of the note frequencies.*

Order	Pitch	Ratios obtaining		Interval
		to fundamental	to preceding notes	
1	C			
2	c	1:2	1:2	octave
3	g	1:3	2:3	fifth
4	c′	1:4	3:4	fourth
5	e′	1:5	4:5	major 3rd
6	g′	1:6	5:6	minor 3rd

and so on until the sixteenth partial

The results in the two right-hand columns can be easily demonstrated with the help of a sounding violin string. If, by exerting finger pressure, we divide it into two parts with any of the given ratios, the two parts, when sounded together, produce

* In practice, the truth is somewhat more complicated: in the light of acoustical researches undertaken by Dr Willi Aebi of Burgdorf, the ratios described here are approximately true only for the muted horn. On the open horn, however, every wavelength is reduced by one quarter towards the bell-end. Thus, for the open and muted horn respectively, 1/4 and 1/2 a wavelength correspond to the first harmonic, 3/4 and 1/1 to the second, 5/4 and 3/2 wavelengths to the third and 7/4 and 2 to the fourth.

the same interval as that lying between the natural tones with the corresponding numerals. An acoustical phenomenon very hard to produce on the horn, though easy to explain, is that of double notes: if you play a low note in normal fashion and at the same time hum or sing a third, fifth, sixth or seventh in the octave above, a third note is generated through the addition of the frequencies of the first two; through the addition of this new note to the original note, even a fourth note can be produced. C.M. von Weber, in the cadence of his Horn Concertino Op. 45, uses a sequence of these chords, which resonate spherically:

C. M. von Weber

Corno
in E

Eugène (Léon) Vivier (1817–1900), who became famous at Napoleon III's court as the royal practical joker of Paris, is reputed to have mastered this trick with an artist's confidence. A few modern composers have theoretically worked out similar chord progressions and incorporated them into their compositions; in practice, however, attempts at producing these chords have largely been abandoned.

Brass Instrument Building in the Sixteenth and Seventeenth Centuries

It had long been known that a longer tube produces different notes from a shorter one. But a preference had also arisen for blowing on slender pipes rather than on the short, massively thick horns of cows and bulls. Moreover, thinner tubes, provided they were long enough, could produce several notes: 'natural' notes, or notes in the natural series.

Founders, who were highly skilled in fashioning bells and casting cannons, occasionally succeeded in imitating a model from nature and casting somewhat elongated horns from bronze. Usually however their skills failed them. In about 1500, however, some inventive minds must have hit on the idea of soldering together tubes from flatly rolled brass sheets containing up to around 75 per cent copper, in order to join them and use them to build instruments. This was possible only with single, relatively small pieces and the difficulty lay in joining them properly. The method whereby short pieces of tube had rosin poured into them and were then bent as massive pieces was probably taken over from skilled silversmiths. After the filling had melted away, the instruments were put together with the help of the small, curved pieces that had been thus prepared. Even at the early stages, these instruments were beginning to acquire the shape that we know from the early natural trumpets and the first trombones. The joints are always characterized by knots, usually elaborated to become decorative buttons, which mark the individual pieces of the tube.

In the first half of the sixteenth century, the chivalric long trumpet was already very common in many sizes, and at about the same time the trombone family, with its many members ranging from alto to bass, was also established. On all these instruments, the bore was uniformly cylindrical along most of its length. It took about 100 more years to learn the technique of constructing a still longer bore which was conical along most of its length and to give it a curved form by means of an organic process of bending.

When this was finally accomplished, the first and most important characteristic was created that distinguished the horn

Buisine-player, after an engraving by G.B. Bracelli, Rome, c 1615

from all other brass instruments: with the horn, the bore has a predominantly conical shape, in marked contrast to the trumpet and trombone, whose bores are cylindrical throughout almost their entire length. It was only in 1800 that the difficult procedure of curving the conical tubes of horns in any number of shapes was made easier. The Parisian instrument-maker Wendel Sandhas hit upon the idea of pouring molten lead into the tubes before bending them, instead of the unreliable mixture of sand, pitch and rosin formerly used.

Nowadays the modern instrument-maker uses mechanical methods to produce seamless tubes that can be stretched in seconds to any conical shape, using hydraulic pressure.

Horn or Trumpet?

This was a question which could not always be answered simply; even today, with hindsight, we cannot answer with certainty in every case. From the foregoing we know that the horn and the trumpet shared the same origins in common with all other brass instruments. The earliest noticeable differences were, on the one hand, the longitudinal form assumed by the trumpet and, on the other, the conical bore unique to the horn. It is true that the pitch of the two instruments was different. The trumpet, usually shorter, was by its very nature higher in pitch than the horn. Yet the low D trumpet, still very common at that time, corresponded in length and pitch exactly to the hunting-horn in D, already occasionally in use. There were, however, other features in common: both trumpet and horn were played with their bells raised high in the air, and – what is more remarkable – both instruments were played with the same cup-shaped mouthpiece. Even the music naturally suited to the two instruments was also fairly similar. Almost invariably this consisted of small, fanfare-

Horn-player, an anatomical study attributed to Peter Paul Rubens (1577–1640) (Musée de Besançon)

like pieces, developed from traditional signals. Whoever could play the horn could also play the trumpet and of course vice versa. But not everyone was allowed to: just as, long ago, it had been the privilege of noble knights to carry and use oliphants, so royal personages in later times laid exclusive claim to the trumpet, with its bright, piercing sound, when necessary allowing its use in church services for the praise and glory of God. Reigning 'emperors, kings, electors, knights and men of a similar rank' retained court and field trumpeters. These men organized themselves into guilds and jealously monitored the strict observance of the privileges granted to them and solemnly ratified. Harsh decrees and constantly renewed proclamations were circulated 'against unauthorized trumpet-playing'; strikingly harsh punishments were threatened. In spite of this, 'peasant musicians, mountebanks, actors and owners of try-your-luck stores' were repeatedly caught and punished merely for unauthorized playing of 'trombones or Waldhorns' in a 'trumpet-like manner'.

Otherwise, exact distinctions were not made between the

Giuseppe Zocchi (1711–67):
Concerto musicale *(Florence, Uffizi)*
Baroque chamber music with two natural horns (hunting-horns); the bells are held high in the air

similar-sounding brass instruments of the time. In any case, a professional *Stadtpfeifer* (municipal wind-player) had to master a dozen or so instruments, both wind and stringed. However, genuinely great masters of the 'clarino' were practically unique throughout the world: one such was Gottfried Reiche (1667–1734), the senior Stadtpfeifer of Leipzig and world-famous player of the 'Bach trumpet'. The portrait of him painted in 1723 by Elias Gottlieb Haussmann shows him holding in his hand a 'wind instrument coiled many times in the manner of a posthorn', as most experts cautiously put it. He did not possess the right to be portrayed with a long trumpet, since he was not a court trumpeter, merely a Stadtpfeifer. Even today, experts are still not in complete agreement as to whether this coiled instrument is a trumpet or a horn; but many if not all of the indications contained in the picture support the view that the instrument in question was a *corno di caccia*. Moreover, it would hardly have been appropriate to Reiche's skills if he had allowed himself to be portrayed with a trumpet disguised as a posthorn or some other instrument. It is much more probable that, as a forward-looking wind-player, he was holding one of the *corni di caccia* developed by the famous trumpet-maker Wolf Wilhelm Haas (1681–1780) from the *trompes de chasse* which had reached Nuremberg from France at the end of the seventeenth century – in exactly the same period that the 'lovely, majestic Waldhorn' was becoming 'fashionable'.

Clarino-playing and Mouthpieces

So far as the history of the horn is concerned, the separate subjects of clarino-playing and mouthpieces are directly related to each other.

According to Johann Gottfried Walther's *Musicalisches Lexicon*

(1732), the Italian word 'clarino' simply means 'a trumpet played high or clearly'. Clarino-playing, however, was soon understood to mean playing predominantly in the highest register – in other words, notes higher than about the tenth or twelfth overtone, and lying conveniently close together, without chromatic gaps (as shown on page 27).

These notes could be used in any way one chose on any brass instrument of whatever compass, always providing that the instrument was of the required minimum length and that its bore-size was such as to allow these high notes to speak well in combination with the appropriate mouthpiece. It is true that these conditions were best met on the narrow-bore, cylindrically built trumpet. It was above all in Germany that this traditional art of professional wind-playing attained a high degree of accomplishment. But it was also possible to cultivate this art on the horn; no better indication of this exists than in the numerous parts for *corno da caccia, corne du chasse, corne par force* or *corno da tirarsi*, written by J.S. Bach, Handel and other contemporaries; these parts still cause anxiety among even the most skilled players.

But this subject, together with horn music in general, we will discuss later. Here we are concerned primarily with the technique of instrument-building and the connected, by no means unimportant, question of mouthpieces.

A cup-shaped mouthpiece made it easier for the upper register to speak and facilitated the production of a brilliantly sharp, piercing, keen-edged tone. The flatter the cup and the narrower the throat of the mouthpiece, the more this was so. It was this type of mouthpiece that became popular with all those players who raised the art of clarino-playing to almost legendary levels, whether in Italy, England or Germany. With many minor variations of shape, but always with the cup deepened to a lesser or greater extent, it remained the typical mouthpiece for the trumpet.

By contrast, the horn's mouthpiece, corresponding to the long, conical bore of this instrument and to its deeper register, was more suited to the production of a warmer, softer tone, and began to assume a markedly funnel-like shape. Thus it approached more nearly the timbre that inspired the writer on aesthetics Christian Friedrich Michaelis (1770–1834), in *Über den Geist der Tonkunst* (On the Spirit of Music, 1795–1800), to describe the horn, in contrast to the trumpet, as 'more serious, possessing greater solemnity and dignity'.

But before the separation between trumpet and horn is allowed to progress further, let us turn to France and to Louis XIV's brilliant court, which was devoted to hunting. There our instrument, still called the 'trompe de chasse', had in the meantime become the prototype for all other horns.

Count Franz Anton von Sporck (1662–1738)

Sporck's enthusiasm for the hunting-horn was to lead to a decisive turning-point in its evolution, when France's leading position in the horn's development, undisputed until now, was to pass to Bohemia.

In the Thirty Years War one Johann Sporck, through luck and ability, had risen from the rank of simple soldier to that of imperial commander of cavalry, earned a patent of nobility, and acquired large estates in Bohemia. An aristocrat through and through, he sent his son, the young Count Franz Anton, on a grand tour. On his travels between 1680 and 1682, the son visited Italy, England, the Netherlands and Germany before arriving at the French court of Versailles. There, as guest and courtier to the Sun King Louis XIV, he familiarized himself with all that was

36

Hunters playing the trompe de chasse, *France, beginning of the eighteenth century*
Detail of a copper engraving by Adam van der Meulen (1632–90)
(Metropolitan Museum of Art, New York)

considered exemplary and worthy of imitation throughout Europe. But nothing fired his enthusiasm more than hunting, theatre and music; and so he was drawn irresistibly to the sound of the hunting-horn – fresh and elemental as nature, yet elegant, musically refined and polished as never before. He heard this sound from the many horns of all sizes that, as well-tuned *trompes de chasse*, accompanied the hunt through field and forest with their signals. He heard horns playing in pleasant incidental music, on occasions when entire companies of huntsmen, dressed in their most dazzling finery, combined with players to add lustre to the public ballet or opera.

Today it is not known exactly what they played on these occasions. Perhaps it was those 'small pieces *à 4*' of which Marin Mersenne dreamed and wrote; perhaps pieces for 'cors et trompes de chasse' composed by the principal composer to the Sun King, Jean-Baptiste Lully (1632–87). It is also possible that he heard hunting fanfares similar to those later printed by the Marquis Marc-Antoine Dampierre (1676–1756).

On leaving France, Count Van Sporck was adamant that from now on such hunting-music should also be played in his native Bohemia. He immediately set to work, sending two of his most able huntsmen to Versailles to have them thoroughly trained by the best masters. These were Wenzel Sweda (1638–*c* 1710) and Peter Röllig (1650–1723), who became the promotors of a new art of horn-playing in Bohemia and the whole of Germany, and the forerunners of generations of players. Count Franz Anton von Sporck himself – from 1691 governor of Bohemia – became a veritable Maecenas for all the arts. He introduced Italian opera into Bohemia, continually providing hospitality for troupes of travelling players in his home and maintaining his own extremely capable domestic orchestra. All his life he remained devoted to hunting and, as the supreme gentleman huntsman of

Bohemia, founded the much coveted Order of St Hubert. But above all he loved the horn. He will always be remembered for the princely benevolence and energetic encouragement with which he continually fostered the art of horn-playing.

From Stage to Orchestra Pit

If one looks up the entry 'horn' in many of the older reference works and some of the newer ones, one usually finds the statement that the horn 'was introduced into the orchestra by Lully'. Almost invariably a short piece in five parts from Lully's *comédie-ballet*, *La Princesse d'Elide* (1664), bearing the inscription 'Le(s) cors de chasse', this is cited as proof. One can assume, however, that this phrase is not an instrumental direction, but at best can be regarded simply as a kind of characterization. One might compare it with some of the descriptive terms such as 'Les chasseurs' or 'Les vallets Eueillez', encountered elsewhere in this score, which unquestionably refer to events on the stage.

However, this does not mean that horns or instruments like horns were not already being played in the orchestra (or orchestra-pit) in Lully's time. But what they played was no more than realistic background stage music of the kind they had been providing long before from their positions on the stage. Moreover, it was often left up to the players whether they played horns or trumpets. From everything we have said before, we know that at this time there was hardly any significant audible distinction between the two instruments. But a difference was becoming noticeable when Jean-Joseph Mouret (1682–1738) inserted short intermezzos for the hunting-horn into his divertissements and Tafelmusik, or Jean-Baptiste Morin (1677–1754), in his ballet-divertissement, *La chasse du cerf* (1708), skilfully wove

38

hunting fanfares into the ballet music that accompanied the dancing. But none of this was essentially new, except that by now the hunting-horn players had often exchanged their positions on stage for a place of their own in the orchestra. Thus the switch from stage to orchestra pit was achieved – at least symbolically. Just as the team of trumpeters and their master drummer, seated in a special gallery at the edge of the orchestra, were ready to strike up suddenly, at any time, with a resounding flourish, so might another, opposing group of wind-players have stationed themselves decoratively on the other side.

The hunting-horn players stood on their platform and waited for the moment when they would take up their powerful, open-hooped parforce-horns or raise the bells of the smaller horns or *trompes de chasse* high above their shoulders, to accompany some hunting-scene or dance of Diana with their blaring. A magnificent spectacle, easy to envisage, and striking to the ear.

The actual entry of the horn into the orchestra may, however, have happened in a less striking way. Perhaps it was the humblest and most obscure people in the land who first discovered and began to prize the hunting-horn as a musical instrument in its own right. As early as 1670, in tranquil Kremsier (Kroměříž), the tranquil summer residence of the Prince Bishop of Olmütz (Olomouc), an unknown Bohemian master wrote a *Sonata da caccia con un cornu*, in which a small horn in C holds its own part within a six-voice orchestral texture on a completely equal footing with violins, violas and bass. It was only a short while afterwards that the 'musician and footman' Sebastian Bodinus (*c* 1700–*c* 1760), in Altenburg, Karlsruhe or Augsburg, composed a series of sonatas in which one or possibly two hunting-horns take their parts in exactly the same way as had long been the custom for flutes or oboes.

But the seeds scattered by Count Von Sporck from his

Two parforce-horn players, after Johann Elias Ridinger (1698–1767)

residential seats in Prague, Lissa (Lysá nad Lakem) and Bad Kukus (Kuks) had begun to sprout everywhere, yielding their first fruits. At first, both small and larger courts in Thuringia and Saxony strove to secure the services of Bohemian horn-players, just as the great European centres did later, including far-off St Petersburg. In France, by contrast, the horn was attracting less and less attention. It fell into such neglect that, when Johann Stamitz introduced his first Mannheim symphonies to Paris in 1751, it was above all the two horns that caused a sensation; they were particularly acclaimed, as a valuable German innovation!

From Signal to Fanfare; from Hunting-horn to Waldhorn

Signal, das ist ein hörlich Signum,
  auch also ein thönend Zeichen.
Fanfare, das ist eine Pièce,
  welche zwar Lermens und Prallens genug machet,
  sonsten aber wenig nach Kunst schmecket.

'Signal' means an audible symbol,
  therefore a sounding sign.
'Fanfare' means a piece
  which makes a shattering enough noise,
  but otherwise bears little trace of art.

These seventeenth-century definitions had long been out-of-date or had become meaningless in relation to the two huntsmen Sweda and Röllig when their benefactor, Count Von Sporck, sent them to Versailles to learn on the new instruments hunting fanfares that were then coming into fashion.

Single-note signals were still played on unwieldy horns usually

Auß Münster vom 25. deß Weinmonats im Jahr

1648. abgefertigter Freud=vnd Friedenbringender Postreuter.

by night watchmen and *Türmer*, or on smaller hunting-horns (*Hifthörner*) by more humble hunt attendants or rough hunting-serfs. Even postilions were eager to announce their presence, everywhere they went, with posthorn calls of varying duration. Their small posthorns, though multi-coiled, were more like trumpets, enabling them to tackle sprightly octave leaps and rapid fifth alternations without difficulty. But in the meantime they had turned their back on hunting-horn players, preferring to imitate the signal-players from the town militias and field armies, even perhaps the much admired army and staff trumpeters.

But the hunter-musicians of Versailles had also surpassed all previous standards, having left behind the simple, single-note hunting-signal long ago. They were able to play from the second to the twelfth overtone and, in the case of skilled players, to climb as far as the sixteenth overtone of the natural series on the parforce-horn, a brand-new, open-hooped yet very elegant hunting-instrument that soon became well known, and on the smaller horns and *trompes de chasse*, which had between two and three-and-a-half coils.

Because it had become possible to exploit a range of intervals, the need for greater skill came to be seen in more than purely rhythmical terms. However, 6/8 time, modelled on the rhythm of

41

Left: *David Teniers jun. (1610–90)*
Detail from Le repos des chasseurs *(The Huntsmen's Rest)*
(Musée Royal des Beaux-Arts, Antwerp)

Right: *Marquis Marc Antoine de Dampierre (1676–1756)*

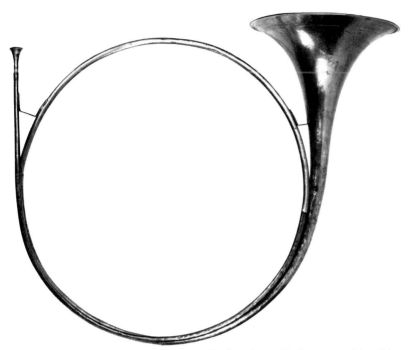

Parforce-horn (Stadtmuseum, Munich)

galloping horses, remained a dominant characteristic. The natural, simple harmonic style of all these short fanfare movements was determined by the almost obligatory form of part-writing in which the second horn made successive intervals of a third, a fifth and a sixth with the first horn; with the addition of a third horn of similar pitch or a second pair of horns, this practically became an established formula.

Despite these limitations, another field of musical possibilities was opened up, one which Louis XIV's resourceful players, along with the composers close to the court, well knew how to exploit. Of the large number of contemporary fanfares, the collection *Recueil de fanfares* by the Marquis de Dampierre, 'father of the Waldhorn', remains a model of its kind. True, the work was not printed until 1778, 22 years after his death in 1756, in Paris; yet as early as 1700 the young Dampierre was known at Louis's court as a brilliant player. In 1709 he became master of the hunt and 'Lieutenant de Chasse de M. le Duc du Maine'; in 1727 he entered the service of Louis XV.

A century later, in 1828, the celebrated opera composer Gioacchino Rossini (1792–1868), in his own inimitable way, composed in Compiègne his 'Grande fanfare pour quatre cors à la

43

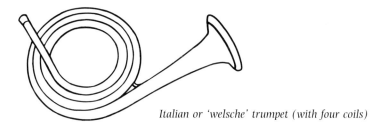

Italian or 'welsche' trumpet (with four coils)

Dampierre', *Le rendez-vous de chasse*, a brilliant *bravura* piece for four solo parforce-horns in D and orchestra.

In 1886 Josef Schantl and Carl Zellner published a collection of splendid fanfares for the parforce-horn under the title *Die Oesterreichische Jagdmusik*. Thus the spirit of Dampierre was revived in the kingdom of the Danube, and the art of playing the parforce-horn received attention that was both new and, more important, lasting.

The St Hubert Mass, celebrated every year on 3 November (St Hubert's Day) in the Madeleine Church, Paris and accompanied on parforce-horns, received a new lease of life in a few other European countries and, among many societies of parforce-horn players in as many parishes, became a regular autumn event, a genuine folk custom.

Meanwhile, Count Sporck's two huntsmen had made good use of their period of study in Versailles. Diligent students surrounded by the best players, they not only learnt all the skills and refinements of the horn-playing customary during royal hunts, but also experienced, and with their alert minds assimilated, the many kinds of music practised in the most brilliant court of Europe. They would certainly have had at their disposal the newest horns from the Parisian workshops of Crétien and Raoux; possibly they also became acquainted with the instruments of H.L. Ehe and J.W. Haas, two masters active from around 1680 and the founders of the Nuremberg 'dynasty of trumpet-makers' who later became famous.

Around the turn of the eighteenth century, when here and there the occasional score already required Waldhorns, a smaller type of horn was beginning to be built alongside the open-hooped parforce-horns, which were too unwieldy for use in the orchestra because of their large diameters. Once again it was a native of

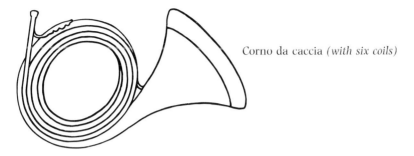

Corno da caccia *(with six coils)*

Nuremberg, this time the master Friedrich Steinmetz, who succeeded in compressing the open-hooped horn so that, while it retained its circular form, it now possessed, with its two-and-a-half coils, a diameter only about half that of the parforce-horn.

But the bore-size also changed. The extremely narrow bore of the parforce-horn became noticeably wider and, especially towards the bell end, much more conical, culminating in a much wider bell. Above all its was the brothers Johannes and Michael Leichamschneider, from their workshop in Vienna, who set the pattern for the development of the Waldhorn from the hunting-horn. The mouthpiece had meanwhile become completely funnel-shaped, and in the hands of a sensitive player the instrument, with its warm, full, dark timbre, was already hinting at the qualities which later made it the favourite of the Romantics.

To conclude, the changes which allowed the hunting horn to develop into the Waldhorn may be summarized as follows:

The single-coil parforce-horn (p. 43) was of such large diameter that even a stout huntsman could slip into it and carry it over his left shoulder in a manner convenient for the hunt.

Around 1700 the brothers Johann and Michael Leicham-schneider in Vienna were the first to compress the single-coil parforce-horn into such a compact shape that its diameter was approximately halved, even though it now had two coils: thus it became a Waldhorn.

Because of further multiplication of the coiling, various alterations to the dimensions of the bore and the numerous variants in the shape of the bell, it is sometimes very difficult to tell with certainty if an instrument is a horn or a trumpet; an example is provided by the instrument of Gottfried Reiche, player of the 'Bach trumpet', in Haussmann's portrait (see colour ill.).

First Interlude

A Flash in the Pan: Horn Music for the Clarino-player

Most of the music written from about 1600 until the second half of the eighteenth century was composed in the service of, or commissioned by, court aristocrats or ecclesiastical dignitaries. Much of it was ordered for a particular occasion or for just one specific purpose. After it had been performed, whether on the opera stage, in public state rooms or in princes' chambers, the music was usually relegated to an archive and vanished on to the music shelves of court libraries.

In the early decades of the twentieth century, these collections became veritable treasure troves of the newly revived and cherished art of Baroque music. Many works from the Baroque, a period or style which has been defined with varying degrees of clarity, were made available to early-music enthusiasts in the form of playing editions. Usually, however, works scored for horns were excluded. Few of these works required a horn, let alone two horns; those that did usually called for the virtuoso skills of contemporary clarino-players. Every attempt to revive these works presented even the most skilled modern player with almost insurmountable problems: the high register in which these parts were mainly written could hardly be reached on modern instruments. Bore-sizes and mouthpieces were not the same; embouchure and technique had also changed radically.

Nowadays, therefore, a great deal of the best horn music remains very difficult to perform authentically. This applies not only to some of the horn parts of J.S. Bach and other Baroque masters, but also to a substantial number of contemporary horn concertos, and even to some of the parts in early Haydn and Mozart that require the old clarino technique.

From the rondo-finale of the Concerto per il corno ex D *(between 1783 and 1786)*

Allegro moderato

Johannes Matthias Giovanni Sperger (1750–1812)

Corno
principale
in D

From the trio of a minuet from the Sextet in E flat (1765)

Joseph Haydn (1732–1809)

Waldhorn
in E flat

From the Twelve Pieces for Two Waldhorns (K 487)

W. A. Mozart (1756–1791)

Adagio

2 corni *of
unspecified
pitch*

From the Concertino for Two Horns and String Orchestra

Johann Christoph Todt *(second half of
the eighteenth century)*

Allegro molto

2 corni
in E

THREE

Hunter-Musicians

On 5 August 1705 Reinhard Keiser gave the first performance of his new opera *Die römische Unruhe oder Die edelmüthige Octavia* in the Hamburg opera-house 'Am Gänsemarkt'. Being an advocate of eccentric instrumental effects, and particularly because he was his own liberal, not to say extravagant manager, he could afford to score his opera not only for five bassoons but also for two of the new-fangled horns. The young Handel, then harpsichordist in the orchestra, and another colleague, the tenor Johann Mattheson (1681–1764), later to become a writer on music, were equally taken with the new horns, which had been completely unknown to them before. A few years later Mattheson, in his *Das neu-eröffnete Orchestre* (1713), devoted a famous passage to the 'lovely, majestic Waldhorn' which was then becoming 'sehr en vogue' (highly fashionable).

In 1717 Handel, now composer to the English court, wrote his 'Water Music', in which two horns are allotted effective and rewarding parts. In his opera *Giulio Cesare* (1724), for the aria 'Va, tacito e nascosto', he supplied a part for the hunting-horn better described as *concertante* than as *obbligato*, and in 1749, in his Music for the Royal Fireworks, he required as many as three horns to play a series of grandiose fanfares in a splendidly colourful tapestry of sound.

For the birthday of Duke Ernst August of Saxe-Weimar (19 April 1716), J.S. Bach wrote the cantata *Was mir behagt, ist nur die muntre Jagd!* (The Jolly Hunt is my only Pleasure!); in the soprano aria 'Jagen ist die Lust der Götter' (Hunting is the Delight of the Gods), two huntsmen played cheerful fanfares on their *corni da caccia*. Here, in the hands of a master, hunting-horns become genuinely musical instruments, not only providing entrancing orchestral colour but also playing a decisive role in the fashioning of the themes. This is even more the case with the 'Brandenburg' Concerto No. 1 (1721). For a performance in

Cöthen in June 1722, Bach had to make do with guest horn-players. At this time it was the usual custom in almost all the court theatres of Germany to borrow horn-players from the aristocratic hunting-music groups or hunting companies when they were needed for the performance of operas and concerts.

The Royal-Electoral Court Chapel at Dresden, under its directors Johann Dismas Zelenka (1679–1745) and Johann David Heinichen (1683–1729), had at its disposal wind-players who, even as late as the directorship of Johann Adolf Hasse (1699–1783), shone as virtuosos. Meanwhile, in about 1728, Sebastian Bodinus, 'concert master to the court of the Margrave of Baden-Durlach', wrote some very attractive four-part chamber sonatas. They are easy to perform even with modest instrumental capabilities – a hunting-horn plays above the *basso continuo* on an equal footing with the flute and violin. At a court concert in Rudolstadt a huntsman was bold enough to step before the Hofkapelle with his horn and, as a proper virtuoso soloist, perform a horn concerto by Christoph Förster (1693–1745). Though this was no more than a short, cheerful hunting concerto, in the sustained middle movement the horn had the opportunity to play with a heart-felt, *cantabile* tone still unusual for the time.

Meanwhile our two Bohemian masters, Röllig and Sweda, had long since progressed to become directors of Sporck's wind ensembles and had also become orchestral horn-players in the count's domestic Kapelle. Whenever they had to play in the orchestra alongside bassoons and oboes under the steward and musical director Tobias Anton Seemann, they exchanged their large hunting-horns for tightly coiled Waldhorns. Often they would have played soft, sustained notes and harmonious supporting chords alongside flutes and bassoons in the open-air serenades arranged by Seemann; as a result the harpsichord

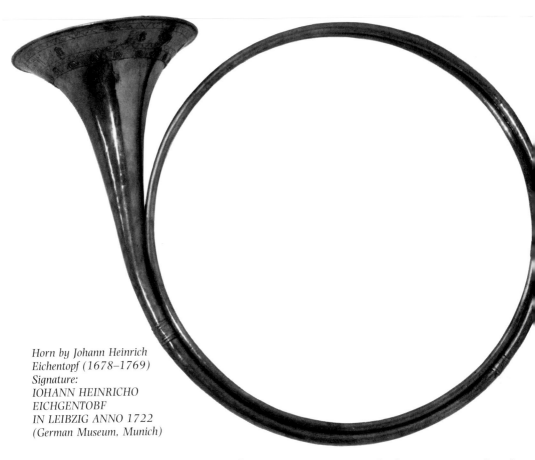

*Horn by Johann Heinrich
Eichentopf (1678–1769)
Signature:
IOHANN HEINRICHO
EICHGENTOBF
IN LEIBZIG ANNO 1722
(German Museum, Munich)*

continuo part, always customary until then, was rendered superfluous.

Above all, however, the two Bohemians became capable teachers. They succeeded in passing on all they had learnt and absorbed in Versailles to young hunting-lads and interested musicians alike. Many forsook their living as servants of the hunt, seeking their fortune as musicians and horn-players. They equipped themselves with the fine new instruments from the Nuremberg workshops of the masters Johann Leonhard Ehe or Friedrich Ehe, Johann Wilhelm Haas, Georg Friedrich Steinmetz or the famous Viennese family of trumpet-makers Leichamschneider, John Benith of London, A. Buschwinder of Ellwangen, J.G. Haltenhof of Hanau am Main or other, minor but equally competent craftsmen; their fortune drew them to court musical establishments throughout the world.

One of these may have been Anton Joseph Hampel (*c* 1705–71). He migrated to Dresden and there applied to join the royal

Mouthpiece of horn by Eichentopf

Detail of horn by Eichentopf

Hofkapelle (court orchestra). He was accepted and in 1737 the chronicler observed: 'Hampel's application was successful "because he could sing on the horn"'.

Anton Joseph Hampel (*c* 1705–71) and the Inventionshorn

In the first half of the eighteenth century the names of Waldhorn-players emerge for the first time in the registers of almost all Hofkapellen – the precursors of our modern orchestra. In Dresden it was the two Bohemians Johann Adalbert Fischer and Franz Adam Samm who were taken into service as Waldhorn-players on 26 February 1711. The two players Wenzel Rossi and Friedrich Otto, employed in Vienna from 1712 to 1740, were still hired as hunting-horn players. Only in 1787, after a long gap, do the accounts mention two horn-players now expressly designated as Waldhorn-players. The Stuttgart Hofkapelle appointed Johann W. Lampe as its first Waldhorn-player in 1715, and in 1718 the court at Darmstadt followed suit with two Waldhorn-players. In 1738 Hamburg likewise took four Waldhorn-players into service, after Reinhard Keiser and George Frideric Handel had been obliged to make do with hunting-horn players brought in on single occasions. The Prussian Hofkapelle in Berlin engaged two *corno*-players in 1741, and in 1756 the Mannheim Kapelle took a group of four Bohemian players into service. The presence of three horn-players is already recorded in Paris in 1754, but it seems that Waldhorn-players were not permanently employed there until 1763.

In the 1780s there was scarcely a musical establishment of fame or standing in Europe that could not boast at least two horn-players on its permanent staff. Already, they had all discontinued the practice of playing their horns with raised bells, like hunters playing fanfares in the forest. Their instruments, which had become easier to manage, were also constructed in such a way that their pitch could be lowered by means of various attachments anywhere between a semitone and a fourth or as much as a fifth; thus, for example, a horn in G could be transformed into a horn in G flat, F, E, E flat, D or C by the coupling together of different attachments to the mouthtube.

This type of horn was used by our Anton Joseph Hampel. After he had entered the Dresden Kapelle in 1737 with his brother, Johann Adam Hampel, the ballet composer and viola-player, they must have worked together on the operatic masterpieces of Johann Adolf Hasse and, a little later, of Christian Willibald Gluck.

The era of castrato singing and clarino-playing was past; the

Horn-player with Inventionshorn, crayon drawing, French, first half of the nineteenth century
(Binningen, Ernst W. Buser Collection)

Monogram (MAR) on the bell-flare

age of the continuo bass was also drawing to a close. No longer was it common for horn-players to blare out extremely high, virtuoso solo passages in the manner of fanfares; rather, they had to blend their finely rounded, soft tone with the harmony of the wind section within the orchestra. Anton Hampel worked dauntlessly to achieve this. It was he who hit on the idea of somewhat veiling the horn's sound (still coarse, always exposed and ill suited to modulation) by inserting the hand into the bell; thus the instrument for the first time assumed that dark, warm, expressive fullness of tone so characteristic of the horn.

Hampel also inspired the Dresden instrument-builder Johann Werner to construct the detachable loops (crooks), which had previously been fitted to the mouthtube in order to change the pitch, in such a way that they could be inserted into the *middle* of the instrument's tube. Thus not only did the tubing attain a more integrated structure but the appearance of the instrument as a whole was significantly enhanced. At the same time, the horn's 'main feature' was created: the ability to even out minute pitch discrepancies through withdrawal and insertion of the hand, as in the case of the *Inventionstrompete*. Perfected between 1750 and 1755, this invention transformed the Waldhorn into the Inventionshorn; the new instrument soon began to appear in every orchestra, for instance that of the Paris Grand Opéra in 1767.

But Hampel was not only a superbly dependable player himself, he was also much sought after as a knowledgeable teacher. For his pupils he wrote one of the first instruction books to become widely known, the *Lection pro cornui*. His most significant pupil was Johann Wenzel (Jan Václav) Stich who, after escaping from serfdom in Bohemia, assumed the name Giovanni Punto and was enthusiastically hailed as the undisputed master of horn virtuosos throughout Europe; he

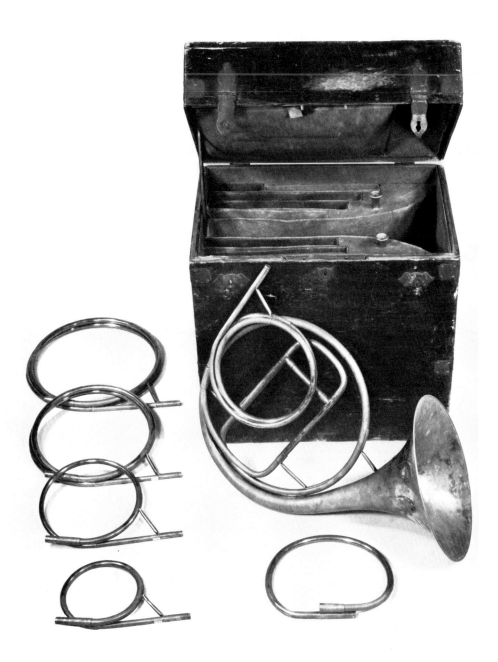

Horn by Marcel-Auguste Raoux (1795–1871), Paris c 1830. With the help of the crooks, all tunings from B flat alto to B flat basso can be obtained. The F crook is attached. The remaining crooks, from top to bottom: E flat, E, A flat, A

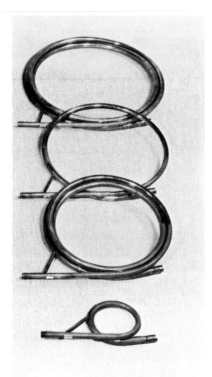

*Crooks from the horn by
Marcel-Auguste Raoux on
previous page: C, G, D, B
flat alto. For B flat basso
the C crook must be
combined with the
coupling device (below,
centre)
Owner: Norman C.
Schweikert, Highland
Park, Illinois, USA*

published Hampel's work in Paris in 1798 as Stich's and Hampel's *Seule et vraie méthode pour apprendre facilement les élémens des premier et second cor.* It contains exercises which already take into account the 'stopping' technique invented by Hampel – the artistic manipulation of the player's right hand inside the bell of the horn – and also demonstrates the 'artificial' notes, which do not lie within the instrument's natural capability. Hampel thus supplied the natural horn with a series of new notes and allowed the instrument, as a 'stopped horn', to acquire a much more distinctive singing quality.

The composers of the pre-Classical period, the Mannheim school, the Viennese Classical period and the German Romantic school well knew how to exploit this quality, which was, if nothing else, a necessary precondition of the numerous horn concertos composed later. During these years the horn finally achieved the full status of a musical instrument and even, in the hands of virtuosos, of a favourite solo instrument. But it was Anton Joseph Hampel who was to be considered the 'founder' or 'inventor' of the horn, because of his outstanding contribution to the instrument's development.

FOUR
The New Horn

It is time to review the story so far. The name of the horn points to its origin, the horn of an animal. Like the conch or hollowed-out tusk of an elephant, the horn of an animal already possesses two characteristics important in distinguishing it from other instruments: the curved shape, and the fact that the air-tube is conical throughout its entire length. While this curved shape (later to become an enclosed, circular coil) is a visual feature rather than a factor affecting the sound, the conical shape of the bore is an essential characteristic of the horn: in this respect the horn differs

Entrance of the Harlequin *into Piazza San Marco, Venice Tapestry (detail) by Andreas Pirot, 1749 or 1750, after a cartoon by the court painter Rudolf Byss*
In a similar way, Giuseppe Antonio Rossini, father of the composer, a horn-player and the impresario of a small travelling theatre troupe, may have processed into Naples. Other members of his troupe included his wife Anna Guidarini-Rossini, a soprano, and their small son Gioacchino Antonio, the future opera composer (1792–1868), who played the triangle (Schloss Veitshöchheim, near Würzburg)

from the instruments of the trumpet or trombone families, whose tubes are cylindrical throughout most of their length.

However, before the seventeenth-century hunting-horn developed into the orchestral Waldhorn, no clearer dividing line between horn and trumpet existed and many early forms may be considered precursors of both. Nevertheless it is reasonable to accept as horns many instruments that have a conical bore, for example the straight alphorn and shepherd's horn, which can be found almost anywhere in the world, the long metal temple instrument of the Tibetan lamas, or the 'Russian horns'. On the other hand, the many multi-coiled posthorns and hunting-horns of the eighteenth and nineteenth centuries, despite their visual resemblance to the Waldhorn, are better thought of as belonging to the trumpet family, as their bore is usually cylindrical. Wagner

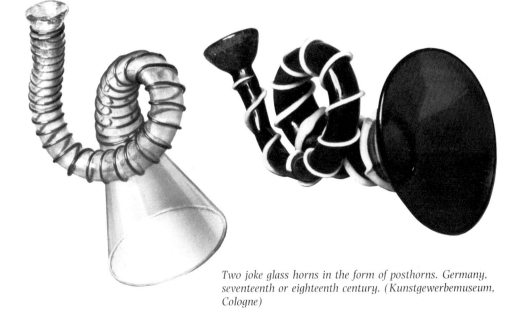

Two joke glass horns in the form of posthorns. Germany, seventeenth or eighteenth century. (Kunstgewerbemuseum, Cologne)

Two Buddhist lamas with Tibetan horns

tubas, by contrast, because they are played with horn mouth-pieces, may be considered as horns.

A third feature of the horn does not emerge until the first third of the eighteenth century: this is the funnel-shaped mouthpiece which, with its gradual transition from the edge to the mouthpipe, differs greatly from the cup-shaped mouthpiece used on the trumpet, trombone, tuba, cornet, flugelhorn and even the posthorn, also on many old and modern hunting-horns.

While the material of the instrument had a relatively slight influence on sound quality, the horn's funnel-shaped mouth-piece gives it its typically dark, soft timbre as opposed to the metallic brilliance of the trumpet. Still, this particular sound is only possible if the player has the right embouchure. Extremely varied sound qualities are possible on the same horn, depending on the constitution and taste of the interpreter and on the various national schools.

The name 'Waldhorn' (forest horn) derives from the later hunting-horn of the seventeenth century and is also used in German to designate the modern instrument. In English, the original name was 'French horn'; this is gradually being replaced by 'horn'. In other languages the instrument is called: *corno* (Italian), *cor* (French), *horn* or *waldhorn* (Danish and Swedish), *hoorn* or *waldhoorn* (Dutch), *cuerno* or *trompa* (Spanish), *trompa* (Portugese), *lesní roh* (Czech), *rog* (Polish), *vadaszkürt* (Hungarian) and валторны (Russian).

The designations frequently used by J.S. Bach, Telemann and other Baroque composers, such as *corno, corne, cornu, corno da caccia, corne du (de) chasse, corno da tirarsi, corne par force, lituus, corno o tromba silvana* and so on, do not always indicate specific horn types. These occasionally fanciful names for the horn reflect a certain latitude, as does the fact that the choice of brass instrument was in any case often left up to the player himself.

Bohemian gold-glass cup (Kunstgewerbemuseum, Prague)

The basset horn and cor anglais cannot for our purposes be considered horn instruments. The former is an alto clarinet, the latter an alto oboe.

Second Interlude

Russian horn in C, tenor c',
about 90cm long

'Russian Horns' and 'Russian Hunting Music'

Jan Antonín Mareš (1719–94) was one of many Bohemians who were pupils of Hampel in Dresden. He went to Berlin in 1746, then in 1748 to St Petersburg, where he soon became a member of the Imperial Hofkapelle. As a court musician he also became director of the ensemble of 16 hunting-horns belonging to Prince Narishkin. The success of his work, and the universal astonishment caused by this ensemble, inspired Empress Elizabeth of Russia to entrust him in 1751 with the setting-up of an Imperial horn ensemble. This had to be newly founded, provide novelty and be one of a kind, all of which it proved to be.

Mareš began by having built a full compliment of wide-bore, single-note, copper horns, some straight, others folded. These 'Russian horns' of all sizes could be tuned like organ pipes by means of a brass tube secured to the bell by an adjustable screw. With these single-note horns a large wind band was formed, the members of which were positioned in four rows, one behind the other, like organ pipes. Each of these long-suffering musicians had only his own note to play in any one piece of music. The parts of each player therefore consisted mainly of rests, to be counted and observed with painstaking accuracy, until the notation indicated the isolated note that it was his turn to play. In this way, not only simple songs and dances, but also rhythmically complicated pieces with fast runs and multiple diminutions were performed. A whole series of visitors to the Imperial court and other travellers in Russia commented on the striking effect of this strange music. They also had words of pity for these living organ-pipes, martyrs to music and to long hours of training. However, the assumption that this Russian hunting music was possible only in Russia turned out to be wrong: thanks to the 'Heeren der Befreiungskriege' (Armies of the Wars of Liberation), it spread to Germany in 1813–14. In the Erzgebirge of Saxony it even achieved a modest degree of popularity among ordinary people as 'Bergmännische Musik' (Miners' Music).

FIVE

Virtuosos:
Jean-Joseph Rodolphe (1730–1812)
Ignaz Leutgeb (c 1745–1811)
Johann Wenzel Stich, called
Giovanni Punto (1746–1803)

'Rodolphe (the Waldhorn-player) is here in royal service and he is a very good friend of mine. He understands composition thoroughly and writes beautifully', wrote Mozart on 14 May 1778 in a letter from Paris to his father in Salzburg. The compositions of Jean-Joseph Rodolphe (or Johann Joseph Rudolph in German), liked by Mozart – ballets, operas and concertos – have long since been lost or forgotten, but his fame as one of the first virtuosos of the new horn has remained. As a child he received instruction on violin and horn from his father. He began his musical career as a violinist in Parma. Only after being thoroughly trained in composition by Tommaso Traetta (1727–79) did he turn to the horn completely and in 1758 he became a horn-player in the Hofkapelle of the Duke of Parma. After two years he went to Stuttgart, joining the Württemberg Hofkapelle as a chamber virtuoso and ballet composer under Nicolò Jommelli (1714–74). Here he achieved spectacular success: thanks to his (Rodolphe's) outstanding example, Jommelli was able to acquire a reputation for treating the horn more effectively and idiomatically in his compositions than any other composer. After a court concert in February 1763 the diarist wrote: 'Herr Rodolphe compelled the audience to amazement with the soft, harmonious sounds of his magical horn [*Wunderhorn*]. The whole company remained in an indescribable rapture while he played.' His art then took him to Paris, where he was acclaimed as a horn-player and invited to join the royal Hofkapelle in 1773; he also received a professorship in music theory and, in his retirement, was much sought after as a teacher.

Another friend of Mozart's was Ignaz Leutgeb, whom he knew from Salzburg as a good horn-player and a splendid wind soloist. His general and intellectual accomplishments are not to be compared with those of the highly gifted Rodolphe, yet he was celebrated for his innate musicality and was praised above all for

Title-page of Ein musikalischer Spass *(A Musical Joke),* the 'sextet for village musicians' for two violins, viola, bass and two horns by Wolfgang Amadeus Mozart, K 522, composed in Vienna on 14 June 1787

his extraordinary sensitivity and expressiveness in slow movements.

The Mozart family met Leutgeb again in 1777 in Vienna, where he was living in somewhat straitened circumstances. In an attempt to help him as much as possible, Mozart's father supported him financially, and Wolfgang wrote for him a series of concertos, which today remain among the undisputed master-pieces of Classical horn solo music. These are the three completely preserved concertos in E flat, K 417, 447 and 495, the Quintet for Horn and Strings in E flat, K 407, the Concerto in D, K 412, which survives only as a fragment, and the concerto movements K 371

and K App. 98*b*, also fragments. All these received excellent performances at the hands of Leutgeb, who was not unduly perturbed by the maestro's flippancy towards him, which occasionally went to extremes. The kind of joke that Mozart indulged with him and Leutgeb took in good part can be seen in many whimsical comments that he wrote into the horn part. Here is the 'dedication' of the Concerto in E flat, K 417:

LEITGEB ASS
Wolfgang Amadé Mozart took pity on
Leitgeb the Ass, Ox and Fool,
Vienna, 17 May 1783

'Punto plays magnificently' ('Punto bläst magnifique'), wrote Mozart in a letter to his father from Paris, dated 5 April 1778. In the same letter he expressed his intention to write a *Sinfonia Concertante* for four wind-players, whom he identifies as: 'flauto Wendling, oboe Ramm, Punto Waldhorn and Ritter bassoon.' If this work, K App. 9 (297*b*), was ever written, it is probably to be identified as the *Sinfonia Concertante* in E flat, K App. 9 (K C14. 01) for solo oboe, clarinet (replacing flute), bassoon and horn, and orchestra. Though the attribution of this work to Mozart has been disputed, the brilliant horn part could well have been conceived as a vehicle for Punto's virtuosic skill. The 32-year-old Punto was already fêted as a virtuoso throughout Europe, and Christian Schubart could claim that he was a 'totally unsurpassable artist who, with unimaginable prodigality, caused golden sounds to flow from the bell of his magical horn'. Golden coins flowed back into his pockets, as Schubart goes on to assure us. But this writer did not live long enough to describe how all the money that came into Punto's hands then slipped through his fingers.

Opposite: *Wolfgang Amadeus Mozart, autograph of the first horn part from the Twelve Pieces for Two Waldhorns, K 187 'Di Wolfgang Amadé Mozart mp. Wien den 27ᵗ Jullius 1786 untern Kegelscheiben' (By Wolfgang Amadé Mozart* manu propria *[?], Vienna, 27 July 1786, at the Skittle-alley) (Osterreichische Nationalbibliothek, Vienna)*

Punto began his romantic life as Jan Václav Stich, a serf of the Bohemian Count J.J. Thun. The latter chose a musical career for him while he was still young and allowed him to learn the horn with the best masters of Prague, Munich and Dresden. He was appointed to Count Thun's Kapelle in Prague when he was scarcely 17. In his third year of service he fled from his master, along with three other wind-players, to seek his fortune independently. A 'wanted' poster was issued calling for the apprehension of the three truants or, failing that, for the teeth of their ringleader, our Wenzel Stich, to be knocked out; fortunately it had no effect.

From now on Stich called himself Giovanni Punto and, as an itinerant musician, captivated the entire musical world with his horn-playing. In vain did powerful aristocrats from all countries attempt to bind him to their courts with glittering offers. He travelled with his own coach and servants from place to place, from country to country, giving concerts everywhere, acclaimed and fêted when ever he played. During the French Revolution he directed, as Kapellmeister, the orchestra in the Théâtre des Variétés in Paris and conducted performances of his own liberation hymns. A little later he met Beethoven in Vienna. In the course of long, technical conversations regarding the horn and its possibilities, a warm friendship grew up between the two musicians. Beethoven wrote for him the Horn Sonata, Op. 17,

Opposite: *Autograph of the title-page and first page of the Concerto in F for Two Solo Horns and Orchestra by Anton Rosetti (c 1750–92), written for Joseph Nagel (c 1750–1802) and Franz Zwierzina (1750–1825)*
(Fürstliche Oettingen-Wallerstein'sche Bibliothek und Kunstsammlung, Harburg über Donauwörth)

which the two men performed with great success in the Hofburgtheater, Vienna, in April 1800 and repeated several times. After more than 30 years' constant travelling, and already near to death, he returned to his native Bohemia. Completely impoverished, he died in Prague after a long illness. The Bohemian artistic community celebrated him at his grave as a national hero and, after a dignified performance of Mozart's *Requiem*, unveiled a memorial stone with the following Latin inscription:

OMNE TULIT PUNCTUM PUNTO, QUI

MUSA BOHEMA

UT PLAUSIT VIVO, SIC MORIENTE GEMIT.

Even today Punto, who was respected and admired by Mozart and Beethoven, remains a lodestar for all horn soloists. For many he is an unapproachable paragon, a virtuoso wind-player at the pinnacle of his art, fully the equal of Liszt, the Titan of the piano, or Paganini, the magician of the violin.

Naturally, these particularly bright stars were not the only ones to shine over the extraordinarily rich musical landscape of the time. But they clearly demonstrated that solo music of lasting value often owed its existence to a fortunate meeting of the paths of outstanding interpreters and equally important composers. Certainly, masters like Telemann, Heinichen and many others, for instance Stamitz, Michael and Joseph Haydn, Leopold Mozart, Joseph Fiala, even Carl Maria von Weber, sometimes wrote concertos for one or two horns; but most of these were isolated, occasional works.

However, one composer worth remembering for his marked preference for wind instruments, especially the Waldhorn, is Anton Rosetti (c 1750–92). As director of the court musical establishment of the Prince of Oettingen-Wallerstein, he com-

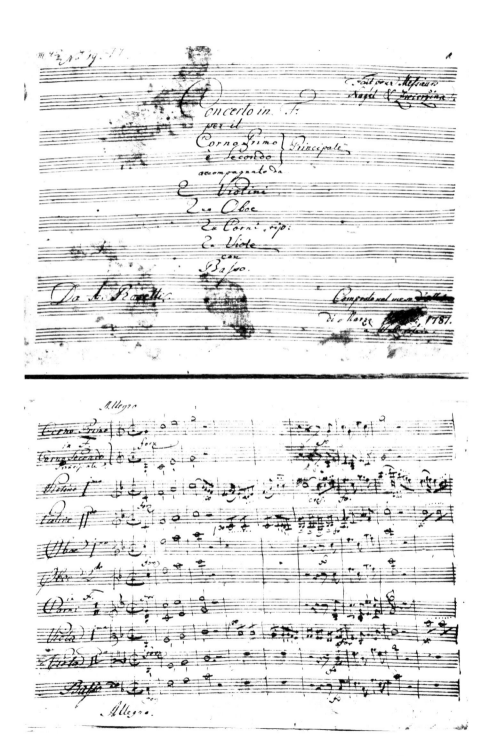

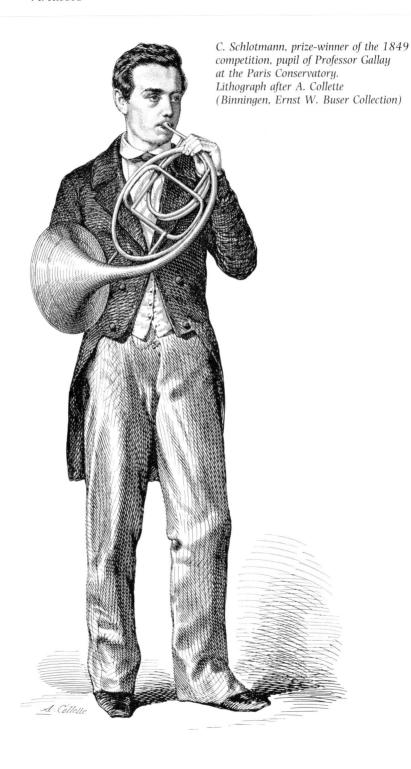

*C. Schlotmann, prize-winner of the 1849
competition, pupil of Professor Gallay
at the Paris Conservatory.
Lithograph after A. Collette
(Binningen, Ernst W. Buser Collection)*

posed numerous horn concertos and several pieces for wind instruments in which the horns are treated with especial affection and are clearly given pride of place. Leading players such as Carl Türrschmidt (1753–97), Joseph Nagel (c 1750–1802) and Franz Zwierzina (1750–1825) also figured among his horn-players. Undoubtedly, Rosetti was frequently inspired by their skill to write suitable music for them.

Sadly there was only one well-known female horn soloist at that time, Beate Pokorny, who was born in Regensburg. She caused a sensation when, at the Concert Spirituel in Paris in 1780, she performed Punto's Horn Concerto in D.

In Vienna the brothers Lewy, Eduard Constantin (1796–1846) and Joseph Rudolf (1802–81), all brilliant players, attracted the attention of Schubert and were also greatly admired by Richard Wagner. The Paris Conservatory of Music, which had become famous, boasted an uninterrupted stream of master horn-players. They distinguished themselves not only as soloists and teachers but were also, without exception, composers who wrote music for their pupils. In the year that the Conservatoire was founded (1795), four masters were teaching their craft: these were Professors A. Buch, J.J. Kenn, H. Domnich and F. Duvernoy. They were followed by L.F. Dauprat, J.F. Gallay, J. Mohr and F. Brémond. Pierre Joseph Emile Meifred (1791–1867) worked with the last three. He was already teaching on the newly invented valve-horn – with which opens a completely new chapter in the history of the instrument.

Third Interlude

'Cors Omnitoniques' and Other Curiosities

In the decades before and after 1800 the simple hunting-horn had become the Waldhorn and Inventionshorn, thus evolving from the simple signal-horn into a genuinely musical instrument. In spite of this, it remained essentially a natural instrument capable of playing only some of the notes in the harmonic series. It is true that in Dresden the highly gifted Hampel had, with hand-stopping, developed a rough-and-ready method for bridging some of the more conspicuous gaps in the harmonic series with intervening, 'artificially' produced notes. Nevertheless, these stopped notes were much less bright in tone quality than the open notes. Not every player possessed Punto's skill in compensating for or disguising this shortcoming. But the desire to build a natural horn with a full range of consecutive notes – at least diatonic, if not completely chromatic – remained for the time being unfulfilled. Many tried to attain this goal, often in a remarkable, even eccentric fashion.

One of these was a musician at the Imperial court of Russia, Kölbel (c 1705–after 1760). With great trouble and patience he developed a horn that he called an *Amorschall*. With its combination of keys and a hemispherical perforated lid covering the bell, it was designed to facilitate progressions of a major or minor second. It came to nothing. Others tried to combine two, three or more horn tunings in one instrument. Thus horns with double mouthtubes were invented – and even one particularly ill-fated example with two different bells. An instrument made by J.B. Dupont in Paris, with eight mouthtubes, came to be known, significantly, as 'Klempners Alptraum' (Klempner's nightmare)!

In 1776, Johann Gottfried Haltenhof of Hanau am Main built an eminently serviceable horn with double mouthtube that enabled the player to switch easily from one fundamental tuning

70

'Cor omnitonique' by Charles Joseph Sax, Brussels, c 1824 The omnitonic horn is actually an Inventionshorn with permanently installed crooks for various tunings. The appropriate air passage is opened up (and the connections to the crooks that are not needed are simultaneously closed off) by depressing the tube the end of which is decorated with a button and which is located inside the main tube. In this way, changes of tuning are made easier (Musée instrumental du Conservatoire National Supérieur de Musique, Paris)

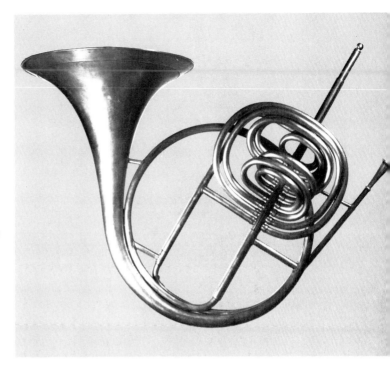

to one of three others, simply by changing mouthpieces and exchanging two crooks in a relatively short time.

The most interesting attempt was the idea, very carefully thought out in theory, of permanently installing inside the same instrument all the crooks then in use (from B flat" to B flat') in order to contain a horn 'embracing all the notes' (omnitonic). This idea occupied several skilled instrument-builders at the same time. The chief difficulty lay in using a centrally located but highly complicated valve mechanism to direct the air current through the tubing that corresponded to the correct tuning. Many different, even workable solutions were found, which reflected well on the craftsmanship of the builders. The first were J.B. Dupont (Paris, 1818) and Charles Joseph Sax (Brussels, 1824). In the years around 1830 the promising experiments of Deshays, Stukkens and Meifred caused a stir; these were followed in 1845 by effective attempts to overcome the constructional problems of 'cors omnitoniques' by Cerveny in Königgrätz and Gautrot in Paris. On all these instruments it became possible to attack or change the desired note fairly quickly and with very few hand movements; however, as previously, for each note sounded only one particular choice of harmonic series was possible.

Moreover, because of the excessive amounts of tubing, the instrument had become intolerably heavy and cumbersome. Though admirable in theory, not one of these systems proved viable or ever achieved practical importance. All were superseded by the valve, which had already been invented. Even so, it was remarkable that so much ingenuity and craftsmanship should have been expended on an instrument for which the valve had already become a reality. The explanation for this seeming paradox may lie in the technical shortcomings of the first valve systems; it was only gradually, after much experimentation during the nineteenth century, that the valve proved to be the decisive step forward.

SIX

Turning-Point: the Valve-Horn is Invented

On 3 May 1815, the music director of the theatre at Breslau, Gottlob Benedict Bierey (1772–1840) published the following notice in the Leipzig periodical, the *Allgemeine Musikalische Zeitung:*

A New Invention

Heinrich Stölzel, the chamber musician from Pless in Upper Silesia, in order to perfect the Waldhorn, has succeeded in attaching a simple mechanism to the instrument, thanks to which he has obtained all the notes of the chromatic scale in a range of almost three octaves, with a good, strong and pure tone. All the artificial notes – which, as is well known, were previously produced by stopping the bell with the right hand, and can now be produced merely with two levers, controlled by two fingers of the right hand – are identical in sound to the natural notes and thus preserve the character of the Waldhorn. Any Waldhorn-player will, with practice, be able to play on it. So that his invention may become more widely known and used, Herr Stölzel has laid his invention at the feet of His Majesty the King of Prussia and now awaits a favourable outcome.

I have become convinced of this mechanism and its usability and declare, as a matter of both my insight and the truth, that its use imparts to the Waldhorn a perfection not hitherto attained, and produces an effect in full-voiced music not previously known.

Although I have heard this invention being used only on the Waldhorn, I believe that I can easily be convinced that, because of its simplicity, it can also be used on trumpets and signal horns, and with similar success. What a new realm of beautiful effects this has opened up to composers!

Breslau   *G.B. Bierey*

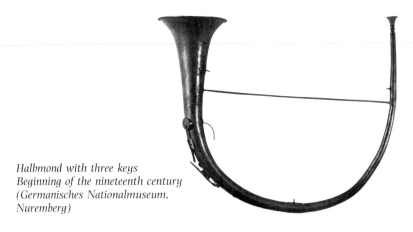

Halbmond with three keys
Beginning of the nineteenth century
(Germanisches Nationalmuseum,
Nuremberg)

This simple report was the first in which a broader circle of connoisseurs learned of a real turning-point in the history of the horn. Overnight the wildest dreams and most ardent wishes of all young, progressive composers were fulfilled, and the brooding efforts of experimental instrument-builders to turn the Waldhorn into a chromatic instrument were rendered superfluous.

The stunningly simple idea of a hitherto completely unknown horn-player also inspired the music director and organist Friedrich Schneider (1786–1853) to a further article in the *Allgemeine Musikalische Zeitung* on 26 November 1817:

Important Improvement in the Waldhorn
Because of its full and strong, yet soft and attractive tone, the Waldhorn is an extremely beautiful instrument; but, as is well known, it has until now been far behind almost all other wind instruments in its development, being very restricted to its natural notes . . .

Herr Stölzel of Breslau has now completely removed these shortcomings thanks to his long reflection upon the obstacle and his unremitting labour; moreover, like many inventors of mechanical things, the correct, suitable solution lay far closer at hand than where it had been sought and was far simpler than had been imagined. He has simply provided his horn with two airtight valves, which are depressed with little effort by two fingers of the right hand, like the keys of the pianoforte, and restored to their previous position by the same two fingers with the help of attached springs; with these it is not only possible but also easy to produce a pure and completely chromatic scale from the lowest to the highest notes with a perfectly even tone. On this horn, therefore, there is no need to change from one key to another, and the same passage can be repeated immediately in a different key; even passages which previously were absolutely impossible to play on the normal horn can now be performed without difficulty.

How solo horn-playing will benefit from this invention is easy to imagine: one only has to think of the eternal monotony of passages played on the horn in concert music up to the present.

Now it is particularly striking and effective to hear low notes with the full, even strength of the horn's tone.

It is to be hoped that Herr Stölzel receives numerous orders to compensate him for his efforts and expense; and indeed every musical administration, every concert society and theatrical institution, every good society of military music and every orchestra should acquire a pair of such horns, thereby enjoying the advantages for their art that can be obtained from such a significant improvement and enhancing considerably the enjoyment of all attentive listeners. For this is bound to happen; and indeed this invention will have even greater ramifications if the mechanism is applied to trumpets and trombones, as seems likely; and any connoisseur of art can see that an entirely new province has been opened up to the composer, as concerns both his ideas and their more efficacious, surer and more beautiful execution.

Moreover, this discovery of Herr Stölzel's has been tested by others, that is, by highly competent judges, and has been distinguished with decisive approval; Herr Stölzel has also received a letter of praise from His Royal Majesty.

Leipzig   *Friedrich Schneider*

On 12 April 1818 the royal Prussian patents office in Berlin ratified the invention of Herr Stölzel and Friedrich Blühmel, a mine bandsman, who had collaborated with Stölzel on the invention. It was then only a short step for A.F. Sattler, an

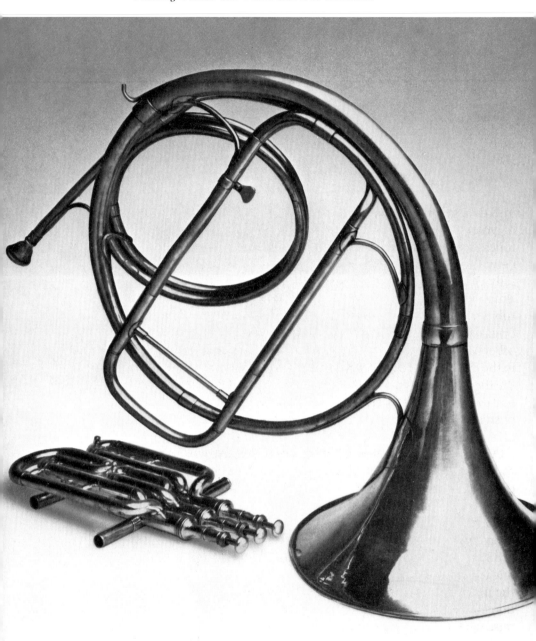

Inventionshorn/valve-horn by François Millereau, Paris. By inserting the piston-valve mechanism instead of a crook, it is possible to turn the natural horn into a valve-horn. Millereau established himself in 1861 in Paris and from 1878 to 1898 he was Raoux's successor. Since 1931 the workshop tradition has been continued by Selmer
(Hans Pizka Collection, Munich)

instrument-builder of Leipzig, to add a third valve action in order to produce a further lowering of the pitch by one-and-a-half tones; this he did in 1819. In this way the remaining gaps between fourths and fifths were filled, and the horn acquired a fully usable chromatic range of three octaves by means of a simple switching device that opened up various extensions of tubing. Sattler also transferred the 'mechanism', which had originally been operated with two fingers of the right hand, to the other side of the instrument. Thus the player had to hold the horn in the left hand and at the same time operate the three valves with the three middle fingers of the same hand. Thus the right hand, as had been the case earlier, was then completely free to make large or small adjustments to the pitch through the familiar technique of 'stopping' the bell.

And so all the possibilities that had been so long hoped for and so keenly striven after were now realized. However, against all expectation, it was to be a long time before the ideal valve-horn of everyone's dreams came to be taken for granted.

Carl Maria von Weber (1786–1826) entirely repudiated the supposedly unpoetic mechanical horn; Johannes Brahms (1833–97) also showed little toleration of the instrument. The fine feeling of both men for sonority and their unerring sense of the instrument's primordial qualities and pure, natural intonation could not easily be reconciled with the mechanical compromise of semitones with tempered tuning. This, incidently, is the judgement that Wilhelm Fürtwängler repeatedly heard expounded to him in 1931 by the choral director of the Bayreuth Festival, the ex-horn player, Professor Hugo Rüdel. An example was provided by the thirds at the opening of the introductory horn phrase of Weber's overture to *Der Freischütz*: only on the prescribed C and F horns do they sound completely pure and natural, whereas on the modern valve-horns they can never be played in tune without some adjustment by way of compromise.

But the free availability and even tone quality of all the notes, together with the agility and unconstrained technique in even the most rapid modulations, represented such a step forward that no one was able to stand aloof from the new instruments in the long run. But if the players themselves, – especially those who were no longer agile enough to come to grips with such a revolutionary innovation – this development caused a great deal of trouble, and for many the adjustment required in playing technique was a quite unexpected burden. One could grow accustomed to the fingering fairly quickly, but it had suddenly become necessary to transpose all the tuning systems in the course of playing on a single, universal instrument, usually pitched in F; this could not be learned quickly, certainly not overnight. So many players fell by the wayside – but progress was unstoppable.

Transposition

Transposition means transporting a note, a series of notes or a whole musical piece from one pitch to a higher or lower one and thus into another key. True, this does not require enormous skill, especially when done from the written page, at leisure. But it requires concentration and agility to effect a transposition, during performance, through a process of re-reading and rethinking the written notes in accordance with what the inner ear hears. The horn-player of the modern orchestra is often confronted with this challenge. Moreover, with every change of tuning, he has to adjust with speed and agility to the interval by which he must transpose.

The hand-horn player of old did not have to worry about all this until the invention of the valve. To a certain extent, the tranposition process was taken care of automatically, through the identity of the horn's tuning with the key of the composition. With the later Inventionshorn, selection of the correct crook (*Inventionsbogen* or *Einschubbogen*) had the same effect.

Apart from the degree of lip tension required for a particular absolute pitch, and, obviously, any other musical and rhythmical differences, it did not matter to the player of that time if he had to read, for example, the three opening notes of Weber's *Oberon* overture or the first three notes of Schubert's Symphony No. 9 in C. In either case it was the same eighth, ninth and tenth notes of the harmonic series that had to be played, whether on a horn in D or a (low) C horn. The resulting sound, however, was either a seventh or octave below the notated pitch, depending on which instrument was being used. The reverse is the case, of course, for the person who is trying to imagine the horn's actual sound from the notation in the score or horn part, or to reproduce it on the piano: he must read the notes exactly as they ought actually to sound; in other words, he must transpose them.

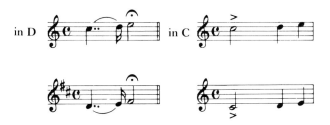

A complicated notational system of this kind was also a binding necessity for horn-players after the invention of the valve. Instead of the various horns with different tunings or the Inventionshorn with the crook appropriate for each tuning and which transposed for him almost automatically, he had to play everything on a single, 'mechanical' horn which was now chromatic and tuned to an intermediate, standard F pitch. Only when he received a part for 'horn in F' could everything be the same as before. But he also had to use the valve-horn to play all the other, older parts, which obviously were notated, as before, in different pitches. If they were written for a horn in E, E flat, D, D flat, low C, B or B flat, he had to transpose his notes the appropriate interval down from F, in other words, down an interval from a minor second to a fifth. Music notated in a transposition that lay above his F tuning, for example G, high A or high B flat etc., had to be transposed correspondingly higher.

This was a wholly new difficulty not previously experienced. It became even more complicated when, in place of the deep F horn, the higher B flat horn or double horn, which combined the F and B flat tunings, became current. The abundance of possible finger-ings that resulted will be discussed in more detail in a later chapter. It remained customary to read the notes with reference to the F pitch. But, for the sake of understanding between a player and the conductor or another player, it is imperative to know if one is referring to the *notation* or the *sound*.

One might suppose that the valve would have brought a simplified, standardized notation for the horn-player and others who have to grapple with horn parts, but this was not the case. Even seasoned practitioners like Richard Wagner and Giuseppe Verdi, for no apparent reason, could sometimes write horn passages which required mental pyrotechnics in order to trans-pose them from the written pitch. On the other hand, the practice encountered in America of printing Classical horn parts uni-formly 'in F' does not, as one would expect, always meet the approval of the more traditional-minded players of Europe. Nevertheless, modern composers should if possible take to heart

From the Medieval hunting-treatise by Gaston Phébus, Comte de Foix: Livre de
la chasse *(Bibliothèque Nationale, Paris, MS français 616)*
A master instructs a group of pupils in the use of various horn calls

Emperor Charles and Roland slaughtering the Heathens, from The Life of
Charles the Great, by 'The Knitter,' end of the thirteenth century
(Stadtbibliothek, St. Gallen, MS No. 302, fol. 6b)

XI.

grauffen von hurn
von gellern
m w m d

des Ruchósier Jegermaister

Grauffen von
Vrack
lauthrach

Grauffen von Vlffen
Crenslh

die her von Welffen

'The Four Hunting-masters of the Realm'

1. Counts of Hurn von Gellern, Colonel and Hereditary Hunting-masters of the Holy Roman Empire

2. Counts of Vrach (the Swabian Counts of Urach, later Princes and Marquises of Fürstenberg)

3. Counts of Niffen (Neiffen)

4. The Lords of Welfen

from 'des Conrad Grünenberg, Ritters und Burgers zu Costenz, Wappenbuch' (The Book of Arms of Conrad of Grünenberg, Knight and Citizen of Constance) (1483) (Bayerische Staatsbibliothek, Munich)

Figurine of a bull-horn player, from a tenth-century manuscript (Stuttgart, Landes-Bibliothek, Cod. bibl., fol. 23)

Gottfried Reiche (1667–1734)
Painting of the senior Stadtpfeifer of Leipzig by Elias Gottlieb Haussmann
(1695–1774)
(Oil, 82.5 × 67cm., c. 1724, Museum of Municipal History, Leipzig)
Gottfried Reiche, the renowned 'Bach trumpeter', who rose to almost legendary
fame as a clarino-player, with a corno di caccia, *as used by J.S. Bach in the*
Brandenburg Concerto No. 1, BWV 1046 and the 'Hunting' Cantata, BWV
208, in both of which two horns are required

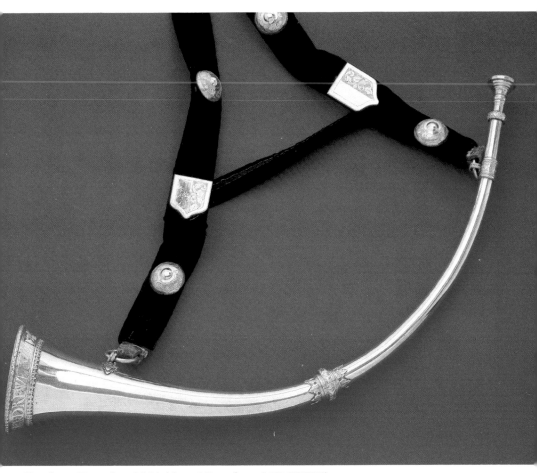

Harsthorn, Nuremberg 1584, 'Antoni Drewelwetz MDLXXXIIII'
Location: Richard Wagner Museum, Tribschen Luzern
Collection of early musical instruments, custodian: G. Kappeler
(Loan from the History Museum, Schloss Heidegg, conservator: Professor G. Boesch)

From: Peterman Etterlyn, clerk of the court to Lucerne, Kronica von der loblichen Eydtgenoschafft *(Chronicle of the Glorious Federation),* Basle: Michael Furtter, 1507:

'. . . *Damalen erwurbend die von Lutzern ier fryheit*
Das sy die Harschhörner füren tün sollent unnd mügent
Dann inen keiser Karolus die gegonnet hatt
Als syn eygner vetter Rolandus ouch fürtt
Dan sy warentt ouch die
So acht hatten wan die nach hüt für kam . . .'

(Then they of Lucerne obtained their freedom,
so that they were obliged and permitted to carry the Harsthorns
which Emperor Charles had granted them,
just as his own cousin Roland carries one; . . .)

*Colour lithograph after a drawing
(1828) of Hironymus Hess (1799–
1850)*
*Hess reserved his caricatures for
members of the Basel orchestra. Some
of them were reproduced in terracotta
by his son Anton (1769–1841) in
Zizenhausen after 1830. The thirteen
figures who together comprise the so-
called 'Grosse Kapelle' quickly became
universally popular and today are
sought-after collectors' items*

Karl Wagner (1839–1923)
Whipper-in with the Leader of the Pack Scouting for
Prey
Colour lithograph, 1859)

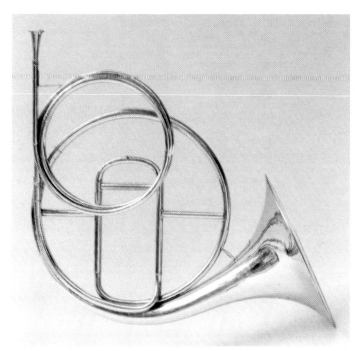

Inventionshorn in C, Bohemian, first half of the nineteenth century, with detachable crook for E tuning; crooks in B, A, A flat, F and C basso also belong with this instrument (Binningen, Ernst W. Buser Collection)

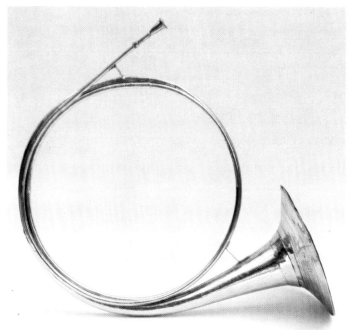

Natural horn in D by Jacob Plüs
Engraving: 'Macht Jacob Plüs im Ampt Aarburg 1741'. Only two instruments by this master are known (Binningen, Ernst W. Buser Collection)

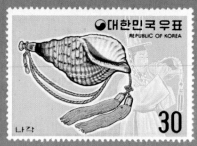

A brief retrospective glance at the history of the development of the horn from primitive instrument to orchestral horn, illustrated on stamps of the world

Row 1: Korean snail-horn, the 'Nagak' (also 'Sora'). Snail-horns have been used in Korea since the tenth century, mainly for military music. Native of the Fali tribe with antelope horn. Kudu-horn, the horn of the male forest antelope

Row 2: Swiss alphorn-player after an illustration of the nineteenth century. 'Beingolo' hunting-horn from Upper Volta, made of an animal horn, with blow-holes at the side and a wooden soundpiece. Natives of the Alur tribe. This instrument, similar to the alphorn, is used to accompany dances and to convey news.

Row 3: Jewish shofar-player. German post horseman, pewter figure of c. 1860. Postilion of the German Reichspost, 1879–1925. Rider with horn, after a Bohemian glass painting

Row 4: Mounted huntsman with parforce-horn. Post horn with cord. Three-valve horn from the nineteenth century

Don Carlos, Introduction

Giuseppe Verdi (1867)

Andante sostenuto assai

Lohengrin, Act II, Scene 3

Richard Wagner (1850)

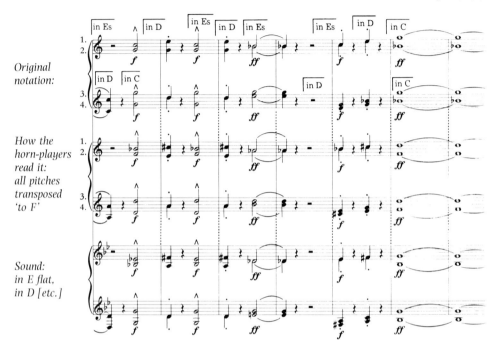

Original notation:

How the horn-players read it: all pitches transposed 'to F'

Sound: in E flat, in D [etc.]

the recommendations given by Strauss as early as 1905 in his revised version of Hector Berlioz's famous manual on orchestration: to write horn parts in F wherever possible and to resort to notation in E as a reasonable compromise and only to avoid excessive accidentals in the case of a few (sounding) sharp keys.

Fingering on the Valve-horn; Fingering Possibilities on the Modern Double and Triple Horn

On the natural horn or Inventionshorn, a player could produce only the notes of the harmonic series in a natural way:

With the first valve, the following notes became available through the lowering of the overtones by a major second:

(Notation without regard to tonal implications, the accidentals being enharmonically interchangeable)

With the second (semitone) valve:

With the third valve (1½ tones):

Other pitch lowerings result from simultaneous operation of valves 1 and 2, 1 and 3, 2 and 3, and 1, 2 and 3. This not only allows a gapless scale spanning three octaves, but also means that for many notes there are two or even more fingerings. In contrast then to the keys of woodwind instruments, the valves of brass instruments are by no means associated only with particular notes. By depressing a valve or combination of valves, the horn-player is merely selecting the fundamental whose harmonic series contains the desired note. Simply through

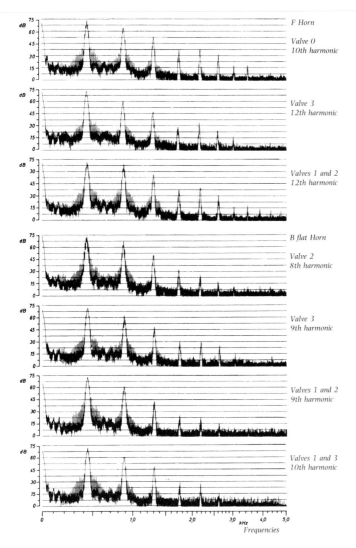

Diagram from Jürgen Meyer, Akustische Untersuchungen über den Klang des Hornes, 'Das Musikinstrument', *vols. 1 and 2, Frankfurt am Main, 1967*

Sound spectra of a' with different fingerings (German double horn)

experience he must know which fingering is the most suitable in any given situation; naturally, he will not have time to think about it during a performance.

The various fingerings for a particular note result in small differences, however: for reasons having to do with engineering and physics, the combined lengths of the air columns inside the horn are not always exact enough, in several valve combinations, to guarantee completely flawless playing in every case. Therefore slight intonation differences and variations in tone colour can occur. The instrument's sureness of attack also varies.

84

The notorious 'split' note occurs all the more easily, the higher the note in the harmonic series. In the upper register, where the notes stand very close together, there is a particularly strong danger of 'skidding' to an adjacent note.

One way to make the upper register 'safer' is to choose a higher fundamental. The desired note then occupies a lower position in the harmonic series, and this lessens the risk of mistaking it for an adjacent note that lies all too near. The result is the double horn in F and B flat customary today. It combines the old F horn with a B flat horn tuned a fourth higher. Other combinations, such as the B flat horn with the descant horn, and even triple horns have recently been in use. The switch from one fundamental to another is effected by one or two thumb valves. In combination with the three other valves, the number of possible fingerings increases sharply. While the simple horn offers eight possible fingerings (including the 'zero' option), the double horn offers 16 and the triple horn 24.

For the player to make full use of these possibilities is a matter of practical experience and individual needs. He will choose the F, B flat or discant horns roughly according to the required register. For long, exposed notes he will choose the fingering that ensures a good response and accurate pitch. For faster passages, however, he will prefer a more 'handy' sequence of fingerings. No role is played by the tuning prescribed by the composition: thus, if the piece calls for a 'horn in F', the part can be played completely in the B flat tuning of the double horn and vice versa. The same applies to all other tunings.

The expression 'making a virtue out of a necessity' describes excellently the transition from the natural to the double horn: the unceasing efforts to remedy the shortcomings of the hand-horn resulted in an instrument that offers a bewildering abundance of possibilities. It is perhaps this very perfection that nowadays makes the occasional regression to the stopped horn seem attractive. Mozart's horn concertos, Beethoven's Horn Sonata, even Brahms's Horn Trio, Op. 40, when played on the natural instrument, are impressive examples of historically authentic music-making. Today's virtuosos have once again mastered this technique, long since considered obsolete, and compel the same admiration as the artists of former times, who took the limitations of this singular instrument for granted. But even the most perfect and historically most authentic performance of any music for the stopped horn cannot conceal the fact that the dubious quality of the stopped notes was due only to the technical shortcomings of the earlier instruments and did not correspond at all with the ideal sonority imagined by the composers.

The Two Harmonic Series of the F/B Flat Double Horn

The natural notes indicated in the diagram can be played without valves on the F and B flat sides of the double horn. In order to switch from one to the other the thumb valve must of course be operated.

The impure partials (7, 11, 13 and 14) are omitted. The juxtaposition of both series makes clear the multiple fingering possibilities: each natural note, whether on the F or B flat horn, can now be lowered by between one and six semitones by means of the valves. Any remaining gaps are filled – indeed, there are several alternative fingerings for almost every note. The keyboard under both rows of natural notes illustrates the corresponding 'sounding' notes.

The fundamental of the B flat horn, sounding *B* flat', is just about the lowest usable musical note. However, many players can also produce the fundamental of the F horn, *F'*. The note *f''*,

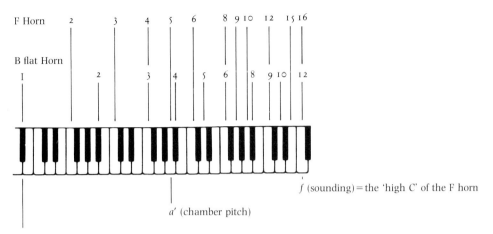

F Horn   2   3   4   5   6   8 9 10   12   15 16

B flat Horn

I   2   3   4   5   6   8   9 10   12

a' (chamber pitch)

f (sounding) = the 'high C' of the F horn

B flat' (sounding) = the fundamental of the *B* flat horn

the horn's 'high C', by no means represents the upper limit, but the uppermost register begins here, and this is particularly hard to master both because the natural notes lie close together and because of the extremely tense embouchure required.

The Characteristic Waldhorn Sound

We have already discussed the considerable influence of the mouthpiece on the sound of the horn. Of less significance, by contrast, is the material of which the tube walling is made. Whereas on stringed instruments the vibrations of the sounded strings are transferred to the wooden resonator, which in turn relays them to the air, with wind instruments it is exactly the other way round: first the air column inside the instrument is made to vibrate; the tube walling really functions only to enclose the air column. However, the air column gives rise to secondary, 'sympathetic' vibrations in the tube; thus the tube exerts a certain influence on the instrument's timbre. However, only the mass, not the material, is important for this process. The greater the mass which is vibrating sympathetically, the greater the resonance. It makes no essential difference to the horn's timbre if it is made of brass, gold-brass, silver, gold or ceramic, glass, wood or even (as was the case with a horn in the Exhibition of Art and Industry in London in 1862), of papier maché and plaster. Rather, it is engineering possibilities which determine the choice of a material that can be worked efficiently at the necessary mass; that is why brass horns are the most common.

87

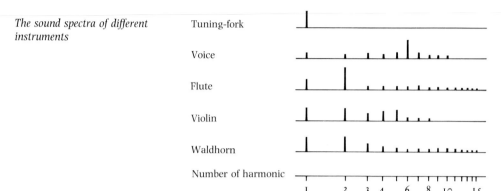

The sound spectra of different instruments

Acoustical details drawn mainly from Kurt Boegner, 'Akustisch-praktische Daten zum Waldhorn', Gravesaner Blätter, year IV, 1960, vol. 15/16, pp. 59–97

A single note on the horn is not a pure tone, resembling that of a tuning-fork, but a sound made up of several notes. Once again, they are the notes of the harmonic series, only in this context we call them 'overtones' or 'aliquot notes'. The fundamental corresponds to the pitch of the note (what we hear), while the others, in their total specific combination, provide the timbre in the same way as the spectrum refracts white light, turning it into colours. The full, warm sound of the horn is produced by the large numbers of sympathetically vibrating overtones. The characteristic tone quality of each instrument can be established by measuring its sound spectrum.

Naturally, not all the notes on an instrument have exactly the same sound spectrum and in fact the horn, with its wide compass, offers a very wide spectrum of colours. Low notes have many overtones, high notes few. In the upper register the bright, sharp notes gradually approach the sound of the trumpet, while the true and unmistakably sonorous sound of the horn comes to the fore most typically in the middle and lower registers. While *f''* (sounding) possesses only three overtones, the fundamental of the B flat horn, *B flat'*, has no less than 20.

The overtone is not the only element that exerts a decisive influence on tone quality. A role is also played by the acoustical processes which occur at the beginning and the end of oscillation. Not all overtones sound immediately and simultaneously, but only after oscillation times that can vary between about $\frac{1}{10}$ and $\frac{1}{4}$ of a second. The same applies when oscillation ceases. The human ear cannot, however, perceive the sound spectra and time differences literally, but reinterprets them as the subjective sensation that we know as the magical sound of the Waldhorn.

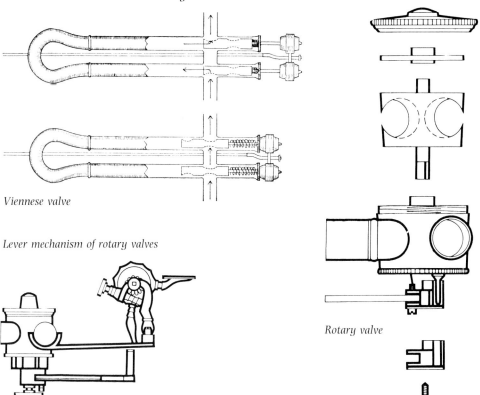

Viennese valve

Lever mechanism of rotary valves

Rotary valve

Valve Systems

If, decades after the invention of valves in the construction of brass instruments, composers and musicians were finding it difficult to come to terms with the new 'machines', doubtless this was because of the teething troubles caused by their practical use. Moreover, there were numerous different systems, from which, in the course of time, three types have emerged that have become efficient and reliable and are still used today: the Vienna valve, the rotary valve and the piston valve.

Each valve actually consists of a double valve: when operated, it blocks the air current at a particular point and diverts it along a loop of tubing of a certain length, before leading it back to the main tube. For this to occur, two switching processes have to take place either inside a double valve (as with the piston and rotary valves) or in two valves switched rapidly one after another (as in the Vienna valve). The switching process itself is effected throught the turning (rotary valve) or pushing (piston and Vienna valves) of a bored-through piston (or pump) inside a cylinder. In its essentials, this problem was already solved with

Piston or Perinet valve

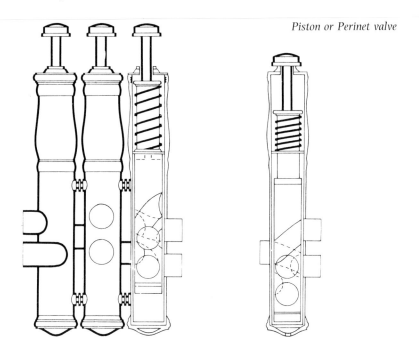

Vienna horn with detachable crook in F (German Museum, Munich)

the central switch valves of the omnitonic horn; however, these could not yet be operated while playing. With the piston (also called 'Perinet' or 'pump') valves this problem is coped with by direct finger pressure on a key attached to the pump. A spring inside the cylinder restores the valve to its original position. With rotary and Vienna valves the action is transmitted by a separate lever mechanism. The so-called descending valve is very common nowadays; when operated, it allows a loop of tubing to be opened up to the main tube. When however the valve closes off the loop, we speak of an ascending valve.

From a purely technical point of view, it matters little which system is used. However, in connection with other construction features of the horn and its mouthpiece, and through different schools of horn-playing, national traditions have evolved which allow us to talk of the Viennese horn, the German horn (with rotary valves) and the French horn (with piston valves).

Viennese horns, almost exclusively with the F tuning, are today played only by the horn-players of the Vienna Philharmonic and contribute, with their soft, warm tone, to the distinctive colour of this traditional orchestra. The French piston valve is being largely superseded by the rotary valve in most countries. The worldwide exchange of musicians, orchestras and conductors, along with broadcasts and recordings, has meant that traditional ideas of how the music should sound are becoming increasingly uniform. Thus it has been shown that the bright, vibrant sound of the French horn, resembling that of a hunting-horn, depends less on the kind of instrument than on the school of playing, hence on embouchure and technique.

New Paths

In 1853, shortly before the living flame of his genius, once more ablaze, was finally plunged into the darkness of mental disorder, Robert Schumann (1810–56) published his famous essay *Neue Bahnen* (New Paths). Here Schumann not only proposed the young Johannes Brahms (1833–97) to the musical world as 'the one who was destined to come', but also, as a mature master, in an act of selfless renunciation, declared his total commitment to unremitting development, progress and the future. Schumann had always been of this persuasion, and he was also the first famous composer to take to the new valve-horn with enthusiasm and conviction. In 1849, in his splendid *Adagio* and the passionate, fresh *Allegro*, Op. 70, he explored the sound of the horn in combination with the piano, making exhaustive use of all the possibilities newly provided by the valve.

His setting of five songs from H. Laube's *Jagdbrevier*, Op. 137, composed in the same year, is a counterpart to Franz Schubert's *Nachtgesang im Walde*, Op. 139b. Both compositions, songs for male choir accompanied by a quartet of horns, became *pièces de résistance* of Romanticism. Between these two compositions, Schumann composed the Concert Piece for Four Horns and Orchestra, Op. 86 in Dresden. Schumann himself considered this generously proportioned, Romantically impassioned adaptation of the Baroque concerto grosso style to be one of his best pieces: the work overflows with poetic thoughts. However, the advantage of being able to translate these thoughts into chromatic horn melodies without any restrictions led Schumann to go too far, with the result that even nowadays it is not always easy to find four horns capable of mastering these demanding parts with the required virtuosity. In addition, at certain places in the first horn part, Schumann ignored the limitations imposed on the valve-

Concertstück für 4 Hörner und grosses Orchester von Rob. Schumann (Neu, Mscpt.), vorgetragen von den Herren *Pohle*, *Jehnichen*, *Leichsenring* und *Wilke*. *(schwer u. zu lang)*

From the concert programme of 25 February 1850 from the Gewandhaus, Leipzig: First performance of Robert Schumann's Concert Piece for Four Horns and Orchestra, Op. 86. A hand-written comment has been added by a concert-goer: '(Schwer u. zu lang)' (Heavy and too long)

horn (particularly in the upper register) by the size of the bore, which was somewhat wider than on the stopped horn. The brilliant Primarius Pohle, conservatively but with great mastery, still played his part on the old-fashioned stopped horn at the first performance in the Gewandhaus, Leipzig, on 25 February 1850, while the three remaining players used the prescribed valve-horns – indeed, were unable to do otherwise. This combination ensured a splendid performance. However, a critical concertgoer, on a programme note that has survived, wrote the comment: 'heavy and too long'.

For many decades this splendid piece was considered unplayable. A French horn quartet planned a performance, for which new horns were especially made in Paris according to the players' express wishes. These horns did not come up to expectation, and the plan was not carried out. Only a full century after the original first performance was the piece again taken up. Since then it has appeared, if only seldom, in the occasional broadcast and concert; it has also been recorded. Even at a very early stage a version of the Concert Piece could be found with the first horn part taken over by the piano. It appears to have originated from Schumann himself or at least from his immediate circle.

Richard Wagner and the Valve-horn's Song of Songs; the 'Wagner Tuba'

The path indicated by Schumann in his treatment of the valve-horn was followed by Wagner with all the assurance of a sleepwalker and with complete mastery. Like no other composer, he knew how to preserve the horn's original, 'natural' quality despite the boundless melodic freedom provided by valves. The themes Wagner entrusts to the horns are always conceived from the very essence of the instrument. The part-writing for the horns, their harmonious blending with the texture, along with the unmistakable timbre that goes with their expressive power and versatility, these qualities exactly match the atmosphere intended by Wagner. Certainly, as seasoned, practical musicians, both Schumann and Wagner, in some of their scores composed in the early days and during the transition period, built up the horn quartet in a compromise fashion, with two valve-horns and two natural horns. Liszt, Berlioz and many others also took considerable strides early on to make the valve-horn at home in the orchestra. Jacques Halévy (1799–1862) was the first, in his opera *La Juive* (first performed in Paris in 1835), to call expressly for four valve-horns. But the valve-horn owes its decisive breakthrough to Richard Wagner. With the 54 bars of 6/8 time that make up Siegfried's horn-call, Wagner portrays 'the hero Siegfried, free and fresh as none heretofore' ('den freien Helden Siegfried in nie gefühlter Frische') and also presented the horn as technically complete in both its lively agility and expressive, singing quality: its famous 'call' begins strong and masculine, full of self-conscious pathos, while the tender central section shows it to be capable of lyrical melody; finally, 'joyful and getting faster and more blaring' and 'still louder', it flaunts itself in its final onslaught on the blazingly triumphant top C.

The Siegfried horn-call is always cited as a paradigm for the superior capabilities of the valve-horn, even though (or perhaps because), with the exception of the section marked 'mässig' (in moderate time), it is theoretically possible to play it on the natural horn. On the other hand, the sumptuous melodic style of the horn parts of *Die Meistersinger von Nürnberg* and the chromatic writing for the horns in *Tristan und Isolde* are quite unplayable on the natural horn. Both of these operas have been judged by Wagner enthusiasts to be the valve-horn's 'Song of Songs'.

Siegfried's horn call, from Siegfried, *Act II, fair copy of the score (autograph)*
(Richard Wagner Archive, Bayreuth)

From Die Meistersinger von Nürnberg, *Act III ('Wahn, Wahn! überall Wahn!')*

Richard Wagner

Just as Giuseppe Verdi, in the triumphal march in his opera *Aida*, placed the normal brass section under a very bright spotlight in the form of the six 'Egyptian' or 'Aida' trumpets that he himself had devised, so Richard Wagner also sought, for the sombre moods of his opera tetralogy *Der Ring des Nibelungen*, a dark-hued family of brass instruments, one that would act as a link between the horns and the trombones. Around 1870 he had a quartet of two tenor tubas in B flat and two bass tubas in F built to his own specifications which, played by the horn-players with Waldhorn mouthpieces, are really just low horns. The bore of the Wagner tuba is wider than that of the normal horn, yet still much narrower than that of the true tuba. Though left-handed, like Waldhorns, in their external appearance Wagner tubas resemble the tenor horns used in military music. Their somewhat harsh but rich sonority lends the brass section a sublime grandeur and solemn dignity. The tuba quartet is usually heard as a self-contained group and its sound is used sparingly, but always highly effectively – for example for the 'Valhalla' motive, to characterize Hunding, and in the death proclamation of the Valkyries. His example was followed by other composers, such as Felix Draeseke (1835–1913), Richard Strauss (1864–1949), Arnold Schoenberg (1874–1951) and Igor Stravinsky (1882–1971). But the most significant was Anton Bruckner (1824–96), who used the Wagner tubas (also called 'horn tubas' or 'Bruckner tubas') only in his last three symphonies. In the *Adagio* of the Seventh Symphony in E major, he wrote a famous passage for the tubas (bars 185–92, between X and Y) in memory of Richard Wagner, whom he idolized; never before had he written a more moving passage for the brass, nor has any composer after him been able to match it.

'Polovtsian Dances' from the opera Prince Igor, *Alexander Borodin (1834–1887)*

Hand-stopping and the Mute

'For echo, no instrument is more capable or more suitable than
the horn.' That Schubart's assertion was valid as early as 1784,
the year it was written, is proved by several light-hearted musical
echo pieces of the pre-Classical period, as well as by a series of
echo symphonies that should be treated with the utmost
seriousness; in these pieces, horns are often given prominent
roles. Mozart's *Notturno*, K 286, for four orchestras may be cited
as a particularly entrancing and curious instance of echo. Each
orchestra contains two horns; the beginning of the second, third
and fourth orchestras are marked 'l'Echo 1mo', 'l'Echo 2do' and
'l'Echo 3o' respectively.

Later too, right up to Richard Wagner's *Der fliegende Holländer*,
splendid use was made of the horn for surprising echo effects; the
'hallo' sung at the front of the stage by the seafarer Daland to the
Dutchman is repeated by two horns behind stage at opposite sides
of the theatre, thus conveying the realistic, eerie impression of a
double echo bouncing off the rocky cliff.

An even better method of producing echo existed in the form of
'stopping', a technique left over from before the invention of the
valve. Until then, the weak quality of the dull-sounding 'artificial'
(stopped) notes had been painfully apparent and could only
partially be remedied; suddenly these notes became welcome for
sound and echo effects.

Naturally this new function of stopping at first required
practice and cultivation. It was a question of substantially
reducing the length of the vibrating air column inside the horn by
inserting the right hand deep into the bell, at the same time
enabling some of the overtones formed inside the bell to unfurl to
their full extent. The result is a much weaker sound, noticeably
more muted and colourless, but by no means less beautiful.

97

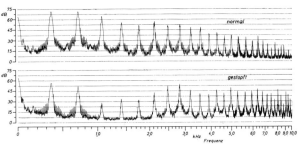

Sound spectra of the normal and
stopped notes of f′ (German double
horn)

*Caricature of a horn-player who
has taken the art of hand-
stopping a little too far.
By Gerard Hoffnung (1925–59)*

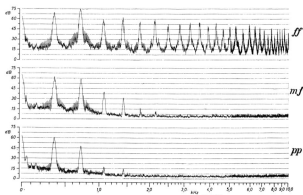

*Sound spectra of f′ at different
dynamic levels (German double
horn)*

Naturally the pitch is altered correspondingly by the process of stopping, which after all means clipping the vibrating air column. On an F horn the pitch difference amounts to almost exactly a semitone. In order to compensate for this pitch difference, the player must read all the stopped notes a semitone lower and use appropriate fingering. On the B flat horn the hand reduces the length of the air column by the same amount as on the F horn. But since a B flat horn is considerably shorter, the section of the air column (necessarily clipped by the same length) that made a difference of exactly a semitone on the F horn, is raised on the B flat horn by a difference which unfortunately lies between a semitone and a whole tone. Sadly, nothing can be achieved by additional transposition in this case, so the player of the B flat horn must operate a further, so-called 'stopping' or 'echo' valve.

Naturally a mute can perform the same function as hand-stopping. The mute is a hollow chamber in the form of a skittle, bottle or pear, made of wood, cardboard, leather, synthetic material or metal and inserted into the bell opening in place of the player's hand and held there. Horn mutes were already known to Beethoven (the 'Pastoral' Symphony, the *Rondino* for wood-wind), and were perhaps in use even earlier. Their form, construction and intended aural effect vary considerably. They are suitable not only for straightforward representation of echo, but also, when used correctly, conjure up the most diverse illusions strikingly and distinctively: the wan emptiness of the Tarnhelm, which renders the wearer invisible, in the *Ring* cycle; the dreamy, reflective rendering of the *Werbelied* (Prize Song) in *Die Meistersinger von Nürnberg*; or when combined with the tremolo, flutter-tongue effect, resembling a herd of bleating rams in Richard Strauss's *Don Quixote*. Single stopped notes, power-fully rasping, can sometimes have a surprising effect, especially when attacked sharply. In *Das Rheingold*, for instance, they characterize with deceptive naturalness the comically fateful sneezing of the clumsy Nibelung, Alberich. But a mute can be used very sparingly, as when an isolated stopped note occurs in the middle of a melody consisting otherwise of open notes, or when a note begins with a stopped and strongly accented sound, only to be followed at once by a cantabile phrase played on open notes. These isolated stopped notes, to be played with a sharp attack, are marked with a cross over the note, the 'open' ones that follow, with a nought. Common instructions, like 'stopped' ('gestopft'), 'muted' ('gedämpft'), 'covered' ('gedeckt'), 'half-stopped' ('half gestopft'), 'with the mute' ('mit Dämpfer') and so on are often misleading, especially in their original Italian or French forms and in translation, and therefore not always obligatory.

The art of good and effective hand-stopping requires extensive and very individual practice, particularly if it is to be accurate and immaculately in tune. It is usually much easier for a broad and podgy hand than for a narrow hand to close the bell in the correct manner and at the right place.

The marking 'bell up' ('pavillon en l'air'/'Stürze hoch') instructs the player to increase the power and hence the volume of sound by raising the horn. It is in fact an illusory trick, calculated merely for show on the concert platform or on television. Naturally it attracts particular attention if all four or eight players suddenly thrust their instruments into the air. The spectator cannot help but pay greater attention to what is being played. But from a purely acoustical point of view it should hardly make a significant difference – indeed, it can have a negative effect. The unusual position undoubtedly detracts from sureness of attack, and it is all too easy for the intonation to go out of control. Nor, usually, does excessive blaring carry as well as notes played at normal strength and without taxing the instrument.

SEVEN

The Strauss Era:

Franz (1822–1905) and Richard (1864–1949)

In 1847, Franz Joseph Strauss joined the 'glorious Royal Bavarian Court Orchestra' ('herrliche kgl. bayerische Hoforchester'), whose outstanding playing and artistic ability Richard Wagner praised as the 'masterly creation' of its then director Franz Lachner (1803–90). Franz Strauss graced this widely famous orchestra as first horn for 40 years, and his outstanding skill and colourful personality were acknowledged everywhere. Apart from being a dependable member of the Opera orchestra, he proved to be one of the solidest pillars of the Musikalische Akademie in Munich, a continuous concert series that his orchestra had been putting on since 1811. For 20 years he was also conductor elect and honorary director of the amateur orchestral society the 'Wilde Gung'l' and, for a quarter of a century, both teacher of and father-figure to several horn students at the Akademie der Tonkunst. In 1871 he became a professor and was appointed a *Kammermusiker* in 1873. In 1879 King Ludwig II bestowed on him the *Ludwigsmedaille* for Art and Science.

His compositional output began with a Fantasy on the 'Sehnsucht' Waltz and a few other smaller pieces for horn and orchestra, piano or harp. His Horn Concerto, which he premiered at an Academy concert in the Odeon, Munich in 1865, is a romantically melodious masterpiece that points forward several decades; it prompted Hans von Bülow, the well-known conductor, to call its composer the 'Joachim of the Waldhorn'.

Throughout his life Franz Strauss remained musically a strict conservative. He loved Mozart, Haydn and Beethoven above all others; he could tolerate Schubert, Weber, Spohr and Mendelssohn, but he was always suspicious of any new music. He utterly rejected the work of Richard Wagner. The first performance in Munich of Wagner's operas *Tristan und Isolde, Die Meistersinger von Nürnberg, Das Rheingold* and *Die Walküre* thrust the composer and the arch-anti-Wagnerian Strauss so often and so closely together that clashes were almost unavoidable. It speaks well for both men that, despite all his musical ambitions, Franz Strauss took it upon himself to obtain a perfect mastery over the still unusually difficult horn technique, playing with such beauty and poetry that Wagner was finally forced to admit: 'This Strauss is a quite unbearable fellow, but when he plays, you can't be angry with him.'

In 1889 Strauss retired. Till his death, all his thoughts and feelings were dedicated to his son's work.

'Richard's talent for composition comes from Almighty God, but his love, feeling and sympathy for the horn come from me', was his proudly stated opinion. No wonder, then, that musicologists have concluded that in Richard Strauss's entire oeuvre not a single note on the horn is inconsequentially or trivially squandered.

In just seven bars the immortal practical joker, Till Eulenspiegel, is distinctively portrayed:

Swaying about mirthfully, in drastically high spirits, he plunges precipitously down to C, only to repeat the whole *Spiel* with added flippancy and mischief.

Transported by tempestuous passion, the second theme from

Don Juan, scored for four horns, is one of Strauss's happiest inventions:

Horns 1, 2, 3 and 4 in F

Many other lyrical, tenderly poetical passages could be cited that would go only halfway towards demonstrating the vivid eloquence of his horn themes. The *Sinfonia domestica* is especially worth citing: in this charming work he portrays in music an innocuously genre-like subject; even so, the listener cannot help being thrilled and enraptured by the *jubilus* scored for eight horns that concludes this idyll of domestic life.

Richard Strauss's individual contribution to the technical furtherance of horn-playing is without parallel in the history of the instrument. That this was not unconscious is clearly shown by the extensive glosses that he added in 1905 to the chapter on the horn in his revised version of Hector Berlioz's famous treatise on orchestration of 1844.

As no other composer, Richard Strauss knew what could be demanded of horns and their players. He never demanded anything more difficult than what he had already heard, unobserved but listening attentively, from his father at home or his successors as they warmed up in the practice rooms. A confident far-sightedness lay behind the composure, at once disarming and encouraging, with which he countered the

anxious objections to the *e'''* in the *Sinfonia domestica* which
exceeded all former limits: 'If it's not all right today, perhaps it'll

be all right tomorrow . . . the day after tomorrow your pupils will
be able to do it splendidly. . .'

The progress made during the Strauss era may be gauged by
the three 'Strauss' concertos:

1865: Franz Strauss, Concerto for Waldhorn and Orchestra in C,
Op. 8.

1883: Richard Strauss, Concerto No. 1 for Horn and Orchestra in
E flat, Op. 11.

1942: Richard Strauss, Concerto No. 2 for Horn and Orchestra in
E flat, Op. 86.

EIGHT

The Horn in the Late Bourgeois Music Culture of Central Europe

During a period when the cultured upper middle classes risked losing themselves in morbid decadence, Richard Strauss had bequeathed lasting masterpieces to German opera-houses and to the world's concert-halls. His art captivated music-lovers throughout the world, particularly because of the ripely ornate magnificence of his orchestral sound. As with no other master of his generation, the inner parts enjoyed considerable melodic independence and imparted to the orchestral texture an incomparable luminosity. The tenor-like brilliance of the horn register, used in a virtuoso manner, never failed him.

None of his contemporaries, not even Gustav Mahler, whose orchestral technique was no less magisterial, nor Pfitzner, nor Busoni, nor the French Impressionists Debussy and Ravel, nor even Arnold Schoenberg come near him. Certainly, they too give the horn some very rewarding parts: Gustav Mahler (1860–1911) makes prominent use of the massed horns in his First Symphony (originally entitled 'Der Titan'). He too is no stranger to the occasional sound of the Romantic, dream-like *Wunderhorn*. More frequently, however, he allows the horn to break in with coarse, crude, even comical interruptions. His tempestuous, climactic paeons, loud and massive, soar exultantly heavenwards, often scarcely unfolding before plunging unexpectedly into the depths of depression. Strauss's masterful elegance and smoothness in handling the horn parts is completely alien to Mahler. His horn parts demand a high degree of technical accomplishment, great endurance and an ability to adapt extremely quickly: in dynamic terms, from the softest *pianissimo* to the loudest *fortissimo*; in expressive terms, from sublime solemnity to cheap banality.

In diametric contrast to Mahler's robust handling of the horns stands the refinement with which Claude Debussy (1862–1918) made use of the horn sound. His dream-like, atmospheric images are magically drawn in the most delicate shades, with sounds that enchant the ear in a manner comparable to contemporary French lyrical poetry. However, one should experience these images on the narrow-bore French horns, with their luminous, glass-like transparency of sound and lightly shimmering vibrato, played delicately in the manner which comes naturally to horn-players in the French orchestras, and which seems to typify the haziness of musical Impressionism so well. To play the luminous fanfares of *La mer* with Wagnerian pathos would be to mistake the image of the Mediterranean shimmering in the sun and the magical play of its waves, and the passionate impetuosity of the dialogue of the wind and the sea for the sombre, menacing sounds of the deadly North Sea in *Der fliegende Holländer*.

Thus almost every composer has found his own language, even for the horn. The strictly ascetic Hans Pfitzner (1869–1949) composed in the style of the late Romantics, in an almost sparsely linear style. At the end of his life he returned to the serenely contemplative sound world of a Classical style that was thought to have been superseded. The original Italian composer Ferruccio Busoni (1866–1924) is nowadays as good as forgotten. His invocation to 'youthful Classicism' and to the 'new law created by chance' of a tonal system based on a third of a tone was bound to fail, not least because of the impossibility of forcing it on the horn and trumpet. His plans, which at first created a stir, finally came to nothing. Maurice Ravel (1875–1937), on the other hand, won lasting, universal acclaim. His art gives the impression of a final, inextinguishable firework closing a splendid epoch in European musical culture. In contrast to Debussy, he did not seek to 'wed the flute's dream to the horn's dream', but allows both instruments to speak their own language. Finally, Arnold Schoenberg (1874–1951), 'who composed with unresolved dissonances', dispensed with the diatonic major-minor system, replacing it with his twelve-tone technique. However, as regards the idiomatic handling of the horn, he changed nothing.

A Modern Classicist: Paul Hindemith (1895–1963)

Paul Hindemith became a bogey of the middle classes, thanks to his enthusiastic commitment to all the experiments of the 'moderns' and, more especially, to the heretical 'Instructions for Use' that preface his Piano Suite, Op. 26 (1922): 'Do not take any notice of what you have learnt from piano lessons, and treat the piano as an interesting form of percussion.' His introspective searching and compositional experiments between the wars were frowned on in Germany in the thirties. But his guiding motto was: 'Even in the wildest mêlée of sounds, sense and order must prevail.' While, during exhibitions of 'degenerate art', passages from his compositions were being played on screeching contraptions designed to frighten, he was establishing himself as a teacher and father-figure to musicians throughout the world. He composed prolifically and was intensely preoccupied with the character and essence of the current orchestral instruments. As a teacher at Yale University, he wrote three significant horn pieces after the Horn Sonata of 1939 (one of a series of instrumental sonatas). With these he proved himself to be as much a guardian of traditional forms as a pioneer in the realm of virtuoso solo horn music.

From 1943 dates a sonata whose layout, instrumental technique and mood are such that it can be played equally well on the tenor horn and Waldhorn as on the alto saxophone. In

1949 Hindemith composed a horn concerto, which he prefaced with the following motto:

Mein Rufen wandelt
In herbstgetönten Hain den Saal,
Das Eben in Verschollnes,
Dich in Gewand und Brauch der Ahnen,
In ihr Verlangen und Empfahn dein Glück.
Gönn teuren Schemen Urständ,
Dir Halbvergessener Gemeinschaft,
Und mir mein tongestaltnes Sehnen.

(My call transforms
this hall into an autumn-tinted grove,
the here and now into the long forgotten,
you with the cloak and custom of your forefathers,
your happiness into their desire and its fulfilment.
Grant resurrection to these cherished phantoms,
to you, communion with the half forgotten,
to me, my longings, in the form of sound.)

It is a tone poem of Romantic longing, typical of the horn, but couched in the unmistakable language of our time. In 1952 followed the splendid Sonata for Four Horns with the variations on *Ich schell mein Horn*. Apart from purely functional hunting (and hunters') music for four horns, this is the first horn quartet to elevate this 'art' (if it can be called such) to the level of worthwhile and challenging chamber music. At best, this kind of music was tolerated on the fringes as entertaining folk-music, but formerly it had often been performed only in highly dubious circumstances by choirs of male wind-players.

In the Sonata, the contrapuntal interweaving of the themes shows outstanding skill; thematic entries follow on from each

108

other thick and fast, sometimes in the manner of a fugue, with augmentation and diminution, sometimes like a toccata, where the sound is at times distorted by means of the *con sordino* effect to the point of being bizarre and grotesque. However, the core of this rhythmically complex and difficult work is fairly uncomplicated. All the material is generated from the rhythmic impulses which form the basis of the medieval song *Ich schell mein Horn im Jammerton*. Not a single note can be found that does not directly relate to the melodic manner and pitch content of this song. It is a masterpiece that deserves to be heard more often. In it, Hindemith has proved how brilliantly he can write for four horns. But when writing for orchestra he sometimes reverts from four to three horns, or even to the difficult art of writing for a single horn. Thus he turns on its head the old motto 'Ein Horn ist kein Horn' (A single horn is no horn). However, this saying originated in early times and even nowadays achieves its full significance in those cases where a pair of horns move in the old and familiar horn progression of a third, a fifth and a sixth, thus replacing the Baroque continuo with their superficial function as a harmonic filler.

Hindemith has shown that it is still possible to be an innovator while finding inspiration in early sources and obeying irreversible laws.

NINE

The Horn Around 1950

By the middle of the twentieth century, the horn had reached its peak of development. Since its entry into opera and symphony orchestras two centuries ago, its powerfully masculine, expressive and warm sound has won it increasingly numerous musical friends. For composers it has become absolutely indispensable.

A third and a fourth horn soon joined the first horn pair of the pre-Classical and early Classical orchestra. This made it possible to realize a four-voice texture, thus producing a self-sufficient register of sound. For many decades during the Romantic period a horn quartet was practically the norm.

But Hector Berlioz, who experimented with tone colour with both sensitivity and single-mindedness, was one of the first to break through all previous boundaries in 1837 with a work of genius, the *Requiem*, composed for the funeral rite of General Damrémont in the Parisian church of Les Invalides. In this way he provided a model of orchestration for the composers who adopted the eight-horn scoring almost as the norm in their powerfully reinforced orchestral brass sections, now capable of producing spectacular sound effects.

Thus Wagner, in *Der Ring des Nibelungen*, requires two horn quartets and allows the second to play interchangeably on his newly invented 'Wagner' or 'horn' tubas. In some of his symphonies Anton Bruckner included scherzos whose cheerful, joyful mood is decidedly enhanced by the Waldhorns. In the Fourth Symphony he uses the horns almost to excess, in order to depict the scene of a shimmering Romantic German forest. In his Seventh Symphony he uses for the first time, alongside the horn quartet, the solemn, supernatural sound of horn tubas, maintaining the same eight-horn scoring in the symphonies that followed.

Just as Arnold Schoenberg uses ten horns in his choral symphony the *Gurrelieder* (1913), Stravinsky scores his ballet *Le*

110

sacre du printemps (1913) for eight horns, of which two play interchangeably on the Wagner tubas. With their harsh, primordial tone they convey the sombre atmosphere of early 'pagan Russia' most appropriately.

With an almost cinematic vividness Richard Strauss, in the *Alpensinfonie* (1915), depicts the menacing clouds and fury of a thunderstorm with a truly frightening realism; among the instruments he uses is the eight-voice ensemble comprising Wagner tubas and horns. With this imposing 'mood painting' we arrive at the summit of orchestral virtuosity and extravagance. To the outsize orchestra on the podium 12 horns are added behind the stage, which, as 'hunting-horns in the distance', seem like icing on the cake in this glorious feast for the ears.

Any further increase in scale was inconceivable. This realization, together with economic conditions after the two world wars, prompted a return to an intimate, soloistic orchestra.

Interest was once again awakened in chamber opera, chamber orchestras and chamber music. On all sides we may observe a return to historical performance practices that were believed long superseded, and to 'early instruments'. The valveless natural horn is no exception: a masterpiece in which we may see all these elements united is the Serenade for Tenor, Horn and Strings, Op. 31 (1943) by Benjamin Britten (1913–76). In this six-movement song cycle (the prologue and epilogue are scored for the natural horn, the other movements for the modern valve-horn) the use of the early horn shows with what economy of means it is possible to create the poetic mood and atmosphere unique to this instrument; the modern horn shows that there is scarcely any fast passage or wide leap that an expert cannot master. In composing his Serenade, Britten had in mind the skill of the eminent virtuoso Dennis Brain (1921–57).

Richard Strauss, in the chamber-music-like scores of his operas

Arabella (1933) and *Die schweigsame Frau* (1935), expects the low horns to be able to play passages which would require nimble fingers even if played on the cellos. Likewise, from the high horns he requires the agility of the clarinet.

The age-old difference between 'high' (first) and 'low' (second) horns is meanwhile beginning to level out and seems to have disappeared altogether in chamber music. The compass of a single horn, covering nearly four octaves, exceeds that of any other wind instrument. Its ability to adapt to any instrumental or vocal partner, and its sound qualities, capable of doing justice to the works of any period, have assured the horn a firm place in the most varied branches of music. In the wind quintet, the 'classic' combination, comparable to the string quartet, of flute, oboe, clarinet, horn and bassoon, it forms an integral, indispensable part of hundreds of works. Just as tirelessly and smoothly, the horn can blend with single string instruments or small string ensembles. Its tone is amply sufficient to balance the tone of a large string orchestra. As an *obbligato* instrument, it makes an agreeable partner to any male or female voice, and in a duo or when accompanied, the horn sound works just as well with a relatively weak-toned harpsichord, period forte-piano or harp as with a grand piano or full-voiced organ. The existence of thousands of compositions in which the horn is used as a solo or as a chamber instrument makes it impossible, simply through naming names, to give even a roughly accurate overview.

Strictly speaking, however, the horn, with its Romantic sound, has nothing to contribute towards the trombone or cornett ensembles of the Renaissance or the Türmer bands or trumpet choirs of the Baroque. But to fill a gap in place of a missing trombone, or to take over a deeper trumpet part, a horn-player can prove very useful if he knows how to modify the sound of his instrument.

112

In numerous German church trombone choirs, Waldhorns often make a very welcome substitute for the tenor. But they can also be very useful in rounding off the sound of an entire group.

On the continent of Europe many hunting societies cultivate hunting-horn playing with admirable knowledge and dedication, sometimes to an astonishingly high standard. In Germany the small Fürst-Pless horns are usual; because of the kind of mouthpiece used they are in essence nearer to the trumpet, signal-horn or flugelhorn than to the Waldhorn. The wide-hooped parforce-horns, sometimes equally favoured, are much closer to the Waldhorn because of their deep pitch. They differ from the historical instruments in the wider bore of the mouthtube and in the preference for the cup-shaped mouthpiece. In practice, however, they serve as a suitable compromise.

After this short digression we turn now to another area which should not be passed over, that worldwide phenomenon, jazz.

The Horn in Jazz

Even famous composers like Milhaud, Stravinsky, Debussy, Weill and others could not resist the influence of the music that originated in the southern states of the USA in the nineteenth century. In their search for new means of expression, many composers eagerly seized on the alluring possibilities offered by jazz. Some of the composers who made the horn the chief protagonist of their ideas were themselves horn-players: John J. Graas (b. 1924), David Werner Amram (b. 1930), Gunther Schuller (b. 1925) and Bernhard Krol (b. 1920). All of them, and particularly Bernhard Krol, have succeeded in assimilating the expressive means of jazz so idiomatically for their instrument that the horn retains its true, essential character.

Bernhard Krol's *Corno-concerto* (1959) may be cited as an

example of a solo concerto in the classical three movements. The first movement, marked 'cool', has a symphonic layout. The second movement is a written out quasi-improvisation over an ostinato, or 'riff', in the strings. The finale uses elements of bop, blues and boogie-woogie. In a second version of the piece, entitled *Corno-Concerto-grosso*, the soloist and the corresponding piano-bass-drum trio are given an opportunity for free improvisation.

TEN

The Modern Horn and its Players

Meanwhile, the small trumpet-makers' workshops of yesterday have become today's factories for metal wind instruments. Their production plants exist not only in the traditional centres of Nuremberg, London, Paris, Vienna and Mainz, but in the whole of Europe, America and Japan.

The tradition of hand-made quality instruments provides the basis for the work of almost all these factories; and yet the cost of a horn would multiply severalfold if one were to dispense with modern factory methods, with their division of labour.

'How heavy is your Waldhorn? Our new triple horn, with tunings in high F, B flat-A and low F-E weighs only 2500 grams.' Notices of this kind, referring to advantages which should not be underestimated nowadays, can be read in the trade advertisements of modern instrument-builders. The results of experiments lasting several years, the incorporation of scientific findings and the use of modern precision machines have made it possible to mass-produce instruments which leave practically nothing to be desired.

The small, independent instrument-maker of earlier times, like experts in other fields, has mainly turned to repair work and alteration. In so doing, he remains in continuous contact with the musician and thus fills a valuable role. It is he who so often executes special wishes or puts into effect new ideas about his craft.

Despite all this technical progress, however, horn-playing has not grown easier, for every new possibility brings an increase in technical and artistic demands. The horn-player is and was, today as formerly, always taxed to the limits of his performance capabilities. Even in the early years of this century, celebratory plaques were issued for Emil Wipperich (1854–1917) in Vienna 'to celebrate his fiftieth horn call in Wagner's *Siegfried*' and for Karl Stiegler (1876–1932) 'in recognition of the outstanding

Above: *Modern F/B flat double horn by the firm of Conn, Oak Brook, Illinois, USA*

Opposite above: *In the workshop of the Rhenish instrument factory of the brothers Alexander in Mainz (1977)*

Mouthpieces are nowadays made using industrial methods and in numerous standard sizes and forms, but many players want the product tailor-made to their own personal needs. The illustration (right) shows the checking of an individual copy of the rim of a mouthpiece under a magnifying glass in the workshop of the Swiss mouthpiece-builder J.-P. Lepetit, Evilard bei Biel

Far right: *The cross-section of a gold-plated mouthpiece made by Lepetit (left) and the usual brass mouthpiece (right)*

116

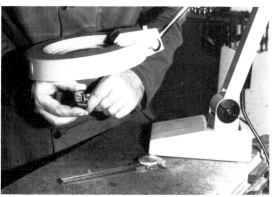

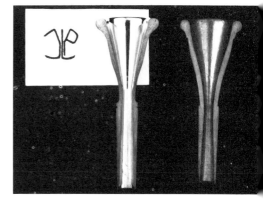

interpretation of the difficult horn parts in the works of Richard Strauss'. The great conductor Arthur Nikisch (1855–1922) honoured his solo horn-player Erich Breul with a gold watch, because he had succeeded, in the course of a strenuous concert tour of the United States, in playing the difficult horn solo in all three performances of Richard Strauss's *Till Eulenspiegel* without any mistakes. Today no applicant to even a mediocre orchestra would have a chance of passing an audition unless he could prove that he could play this and many other passages flawlessly, at each repetition.

Turning our attention now to the phenomenon of the modern travelling virtuoso, we cannot avoid thinking of the prototype of them all, who stood at the height of his fame in the last quarter of the eighteenth century: Giovanni Punto. It is true that he was neither the first or the only solo horn-player. He must, however, have been by far the most important, supreme in musical qualities and technical perfection. He was also the one who by all accounts obtained by far the greatest success in both artistic and material terms. His inestimable advantage lay in his complete self-reliance and independence. He lived at a time when a proto-Romantically effusive society threw open its doors to greet travelling folk and delighted in holding both heart and purse open to itinerant artists especially virtuoso musicians. His fame eclipsed all contemporary horn-players, among them Johann Palsa (1754–92), Jean Lebrun (1759–1809), Luigi Belloli (1770–1817), the brothers Ignaz and Anton Boeck (1754/7–after 1815), Joseph and Peter Petrides (1755/60–after 1824) and many, many others.

Almost 150 years of intensely busy music history were to elapse before another star of Punto's greatness and radiance dawned on the horizon. This was Dennis Brain (1921–57). Benjamin Britten, Elisabeth Lutyens, G. Bryan, Gordon Jacob and

Paul Hindemith were all enthusiastic about his art and wrote important horn concertos or virtuoso solo pieces for him. But in the course of his all-too-short life (he was killed at the age of 36 in a car accident), the world had changed. A whole series of new names had emerged. A few particularly gifted players might have been able to compete with Brain as a soloist on the concert platform. But fewer and fewer of them could afford to free themselves from the ties of an economically secure position in one of the top orchestras and lead the independent life of a soloist. At the same time, mass media such as radio and recordings were already capable of carrying the artistry of these master players to the most remote corners of the planet.

Perhaps we are suffering from an over-dose of perfection, a surfeit of virtuoso sensation, whereby the most difficult music is tossed off with apparent ease; or perhaps it is just a certain nostalgia that explains the present-day return to the early natural horn, which has long fallen out of use. The renunciation of an all-too-perfect technique has possibly restored our contact with the human strivings and achievements of the artists including those of earlier periods. In any case, the momentum of this practice cannot and should not be checked.

It is hardly possible to mention by name all the important horn-players of today and hope to do even approximate justice to them. Therefore the players named below may be considered as simply representing some at least of the prominent characteristics of the schools of their respective countries, the playing styles of which are subject to national influences.

For Germany we may mention Hermann Baumann and Peter Damm. As well as their activities as teachers and as worldwide soloists, both have earned acclaim for their revival of the natural horn and of the virtuoso technique of hand-stopping. Nor should we forget players like Hans Noeth, Wilhelm Krüger or Fritz Huth,

Orchestral horn-player

who as gifted teachers have trained entire generations of horn-players in the last few decades. The same applies to Josef Veleba of Vienna and Lucien Thévet of Paris. Georges Barboteu is preoccupied with bringing his specifically French conception of the ideal horn sound nearer to other schools of horn-playing.

In Switzerland, Edmond Leloir and József Molnár work; the latter may be credited with having introduced the alphorn into the concert-hall. The Italian school is represented by Domenico Ceccarossi. Adriaan van Woudenberg may be mentioned for the Netherlands, Frøydis Ree Wekre for Norway, Ib Lanzky-Otto for Sweden and Holger Fransman for Finland. Russian sensibility and ideals are represented by Vitali Buyanovsky. František Šolc in Czechoslovakia and Paul Staicu in Romania may round off the list for the continent.

Alan Civil and Barry Tuckwell represent the United Kingdom. Tuckwell, born in Australia, began his career when he was only 14 years old and, like Hermann Baumann, may be counted among the rare breed of players who – in the wake of Giovanni Punto and Dennis Brain – appear exclusively as soloists. They each have a workload of about 150 to 200 concerts, broadcasts and recordings a year.

Several Europeans set their stamp on American concert life. Max Hess, Anton Horner, Max Pottag and Lorenzo Sansone should be named merely by way of example. One of the leading horn teachers in the United States is Philip Farkas. Mason Jones and Harold Meek may also be mentioned as long-serving soloists with leading American orchestras. Alexander J. Grieve in Australia and Chiyo Matsubara in Japan conclude this excellent parade. They are all known to music-lovers worldwide through their numerous recordings, work or have worked as teachers or adjudicators and have enriched the horn literature with new textbooks and other modern study material.

The very high early reputation of the horn classes of the Paris Conservatory or the 'Conservatory of Europe' in Prague is nowadays shared by a whole series of truly magnificent colleges and conservatories. Throughout Europe, as also in the New World, many progressive teaching talents are preoccupied with up-and-coming players. Many age-old prejudices have disappeared – for a long time it has not been considered at all demeaning to play 'merely' second fiddle or 'merely' third or fourth horn.

Unfortunately a large part of the concert-going public still concentrate overwhelmingly on the conductor or soloists, and all too easily the orchestral player disappears into the anonymity of the large ensemble. But the wind-player, whichever part he is playing in the orchestra, is still more or less of a 'soloist', unlike the *tutti* string-players. Not only the leader of the horn section, the horn soloist, but also the other members of his group must occasionally play important passages singly, or together in twos, threes or fours, thereby suddenly stepping out of their accompaniment role. Often enough such solo passages are suddenly projected into the foreground of the musical argument, and sometimes, as regards virtuosity, they bear comparison with any solo concerto. Each player is responsible for shaping his own individual part but must nevertheless submit, with an artist's discipline, to the collectivity of the orchestra, the shaping will of the conductor and the creative wishes of the composer.

The literature that occasions all this effort should also make it worthwhile. This is undoubtedly the case with all the masterpieces that we cherish as the most precious treasures of our cultural heritage. But every living art must constantly renew itself; even music must not be allowed to stand still.

And so, today as in the past, composers with a varying sense of vocation produce 'new music'. Many of them attempt to do so with novel means. Electronics permit a boundless expansion of our traditional sound world. New notational methods are devised, scores and parts written which, with their many symbolical signs, are to be regarded by the performers simply as a kind of guide for use in a free improvisation. This more or less consistently aleatorical style invites a kind of improvisation that forms part of the composition and the unpredictable play of chance. When such a piece has opened, even the musicians do not often know how it will continue or even how it will end. So the future is uncertain. What is certain is that it is still possible – and many an example proves it – to write moving, stirring compositions, even to break new ground, yet remain within a traditional style.

Today we do not know how future composers will shape their music. But it is quite certain that enough horns and players will be found all over the world ready and able to offer this new art, whatever it might be, to music-lovers everywhere.

List of Photographs

Index

Index

• THE •
BATSFORD
MUSICAL
INSTRUMENT
SERIES

THE FLUTE
Raymond Meylan

An informative combination of historical detail, key personalities and practical advice for amateur flautists, students and the general reader, with numerous musical examples, diagrams and illustrations.

0 7134 5737 6 ● hardback
● 30 colour and black & white photographs ● 26 line drawings and music examples

THE OBOE AND THE BASSOON
Gunther Joppig

A detailed account of these double reed instruments, their relations, history, orchestral role, exponents and repertoire. The author includes modern trends in the making and playing of the oboe and bassoon; and, being a proficient player of these and other wind instruments, gives useful advice to those learning to play them.

0 7134 5680 9 ● hardback
● over 50 colour and black & white photographs ● 85 line drawings and music examples

THE TRUMPET
Edward Tarr

A concise introduction to the trumpet and its history with a wealth of illustrative material. Technical questions for the player and for the instrument maker are carefully explained. Throughout the book, there is reference to major works and key personalities.

0 7134 5463 6 ● hardback
● over 20 colour and black & white photographs ● 57 line drawings and music examples

THE HORN
Kurt Janetzky & Bernhard Brüchle

A comprehensive record of all aspects of the horn including its origins, technical developments, variants, virtuosi, and place in the repertoire.

0 7134 5681 7 ● hardback ● 18 colour and black & white photographs ● 70 line drawings and music examples